W9-BWC-850

# Reconnecting to Work

# Reconnecting to Work

## Policies to Mitigate Long-Term Unemployment and Its Consequences

Lauren D. Appelbaum
*Editor*

2012

W.E. Upjohn Institute for Employment Research
Kalamazoo, Michigan

**Library of Congress Cataloging-in-Publication Data**

Reconnecting to work : policies to mitigate long-term unemployment and its consequences / Lauren D. Appelbaum, editor.
  p. cm.
  Papers presented at a conference held on Apr. 1–2, 2011.
  Includes bibliographical references and index.
  ISBN-13: 978-0-88099-406-4 (pbk. : alk. paper)
  ISBN-10: 0-88099-406-1 (pbk. : alk. paper)
  ISBN-13: 978-0-88099-408-8 (hardcover : alk. paper)
  ISBN-10: 0-88099-408-8 (hardcover : alk. paper)
  1. Labor policy—United States—Congresses. 2. Unemployment—United States—Congresses. 3. Full employment policies—United States—Congresses. 4. Recessions—United States—Congresses. I. Appelbaum, Lauren D.
  HD5724.R337 2012
  331.13'770973—dc23
                        2012034390

The facts presented in this study and the observations and viewpoints expressed are the sole responsibility of the authors. They do not necessarily represent positions of the W.E. Upjohn Institute for Employment Research.

Cover design by Alcorn Publication Design.
Index prepared by Diane Worden.
Printed in the United States of America.
Printed on recycled paper.

# Contents

Foreword: What Happened to Shared Prosperity and Full Employment    vii
and How to Get Them Back: A Seussian Perspective
*Richard B. Freeman*

1   **Introduction**     1
    *Lauren D. Appelbaum*

2   **Job Displacements in Recessions: An Overview of Long-Term**    17
    **Consequences and Policy Options**
    *Till von Wachter*

3   **Labor Market Policy in the Great Recession: Lessons from**    37
    **Denmark and Germany**
    *John Schmitt*

4   **Causality in the Relationship between Mental Health**    63
    **and Unemployment**
    *Timothy M. Diette, Arthur H. Goldsmith, Darrick Hamilton, and*
    *William Darity Jr.*

5   **Work Together to Let Everyone Work: A Study of the**    95
    **Cooperative Job-Placement Effort in the Netherlands**
    *Hilbrand Oldenhuis and Louis Polstra*

6   **Stabilizing Employment: The Role of Short-Time Compensation**    113
    *Vera Brusentsev and Wayne Vroman*

7   **Labor Market Measures in the Crisis and the Convergence of**    137
    **Social Models**
    *Michele Tiraboschi and Silvia Spattini*

Authors    167

Index    169

About the Institute    179

# Foreword

## What Happened to Shared Prosperity and Full Employment and How to Get Them Back: A Seussian Perspective

Richard B. Freeman
*Harvard University and*
*National Bureau of Economic Research*

The conference "Reconnecting to Work" was held on April 1–2, 2011, as the United States suffered its worst job market since the Great Depression. Reconnecting to work, indeed! With 9–10 percent unemployment and little sign of substantive job growth in the foreseeable future, American workers needed more help to find work than at any time since the 1930s. Even if job growth were to miraculously pick up, most workers would have trouble keeping their heads above water for years to come. For nearly four decades the benefits of economic growth have gone almost entirely to a small sliver of wealthy Americans. The vast bulk of workers struggled with stagnant real wages and high consumer debt to remain in the middle class. Inequality rose to levels off the map for a major advanced country and exceeded levels in most third-world countries. Contrary to what many Americans believe, social mobility in the United States was below that for most other advanced countries.[1]

Something or someone had taken shared prosperity and full employment from the American people. Something or someone was dismantling the road to the middle class on which the United States was built, and with it the American dream. Who or what could that be?

The first place where economists seek an answer to changes in economic outcomes is in the operation of markets. Viewing the U.S. labor market as highly competitive and responsive to market forces, some economists explain the stagnation of real wages in terms of (unmeasured) technologically driven shifts in demand for labor that favor the highly skilled over the less skilled. But changes in skill premium explain only a small proportion of increased inequality. Most of the rise in inequality occurs within observationally equivalent groups—among persons with the same age, gender, race, education, math and literacy test scores, and so on—rather than across skill groups. And it is difficult to understand why in a highly flexible job market firms cut employment rapidly in recession but failed to increase employment in the ensuing recovery. To fit the observed pattern of change, analysts must go beyond the basic flexible market model to consider institutions, unions, executive compensation, modes of corporate governance, and governmental policies.

In the spirit of the interdisciplinary Reconnecting to Work conference, I explored what other social sciences said about the loss of shared prosperity and jobs crisis. Sociology focuses on the behavior of the poor and the measurement/meaning of class but also offers network analysis that quantifies the connections among the elite. Political science documents the importance of lobbying in determining the rules that govern how markets operate and of the revolving door between public service and lobbying activities. Social psychology shows how readily authority figures and settings can influence people to behave with little regard to others even without monetary incentives. But neither economics nor the other social sciences gave me the overarching vision or narrative about who or what was undoing the U.S. middle class.

With the time for my presentation at the conference growing short, I widened my search. As a youth I read widely in literature, from the Greek tragedies to Alice in Wonderland to Charles Bukowski. Did the world of literature offer an analogy or a clue to the story? Eureka! Yes, there was one narrative that seemed to provide insight into the economics of lost prosperity and jobs, and it was by the world's most famous and accomplished writer and poet of children's verse—Dr. Seuss, master of the trisyllabic meter.

Dr. Seuss? Many of the experts at the conference would recall *The Cat in the Hat* (1957a) and wonder what hat I was wearing when Seuss popped into my head as offering a framework for understanding the country's economic woes. Hopefully the evidence would convince them (and you), as it convinced me, that the answer to who stole American prosperity and full employment lies in the classic Seuss tale *How the Grinch Stole Christmas* (1957b) and its successor stories.

# THE GRINCHES OF WALL STREET

The *Grinch* is an illustrated book. Rereading your copy, you will surely notice, as I did, the uncanny resemblance of the illustrations of the snarly heartless cave-dwelling Grinch to the bankers, mortgage brokers, and Wall Street–dwelling financiers who sold "liars' loans" to Americans seeking home ownership, sliced and diced mortgages to hide the risks to investors seeking safe assets, created credit default swaps and exotic derivatives that paid if businesses collapsed or people absconded on debts, and sold clients financial products that they believed would fail. Those dark brows, sour Grinchy grin, and piercing eyes—if the Grinch were a bit pudgier or Bernard Madoff a bit leaner, they'd be kissing cousins.

So who plays the Grinch in the U.S. economy? According to the Wall Street occupiers, it is the upper 1 percent of the income distribution. More accurately, it is the upper 0.1 percent that gained essentially all of the economic growth of the past 40 years. In 1970 the top 0.1 percent in income had 2.7 percent of national income. Their income was 27 times the mean income. In 2007 the top 0.1 percent had 12.3 percent of national income.[2] Their income was 123 times the mean. But these figures understate the disparity in income between the top 0.1 percent and the average American. The average includes the income of the top 0.1 percent. Comparing the income of those in the top 0.1 percent with the income of those in the bottom 99.9 percent raises the estimated ratio to 140 times in 2007. Moreover, income distributions are "right-skewed" so that a person in the median of the income distribution makes less than the average. In 2007 the median income of families was 77.8 percent of the mean income in the United States, suggesting that the income of the upper 0.1 percent was on the order of 180 times the median income (U.S. Census Bureau 2011, Table F-8).

Who, you may ask, comprises the upper 0.1 percent? Bakija, Cole, and Heim (2010, Table 3) find that in 2005, about 64 percent of the top 0.1 percent were executives, managers, supervisors, and financial professionals, or worked in real estate. The 403 or so billionaires in the annual Forbes list are there. The top corporate executives and Wall Street bankers are there. Following the 1999 repeal of the Glass-Steagall Act provisions that separated commercial banks that hold deposits from the riskier investment banks that issue securities, the finance sector expanded. Finance absorbed a disproportionate 40 percent of business profits. It hired some of the country's best and brightest to develop new financial instruments, which it peddled as essentially risk free, all the while enveloping the real economy with a highly leveraged financial house of cards—an estimated $22 of derivatives for every dollar of goods and services produced in 2009 (Matai 2009)!

While some high-income recipients made their money primarily through salaries, for many, million-dollar salaries were chump change, dwarfed by earnings from stock options or restricted shares that gave them ownership claims on the firm or by bonuses paid as incentive pay. When the firm's share price rises, the owners of the options and shares benefit even if the price rise was due to factors outside their control. When the stock market crashed after the 9/11 terrorist attacks, some firms gave out new options at the abnormally low market prices, which paid off handsomely when the market recovered. In general, when share prices fall and drive options "under water," boards of directors give out new options at the low prices to "reincentivize" executives. At the top of the income distribution, the IRS reports that the 400 persons with the highest adjusted gross income earned 10 percent of all capital gains, 4 percent of all interest, and 4 percent of all dividends received in the United States in 2007 (Mi2g 2009). Great ways to make a living if you can get it.

The implosion of Wall Street and ensuing recession affected the entire economy. The federal government bailed out the banks with Troubled Asset Relief Program (TARP) monies. The Federal Reserve loaned $1.2 trillion dollars to the banks to help them recapitalize. The Obama administration's stimulus package—tax cuts, support of state and local governments, and spending initiatives—helped the economy recover while adding to the federal deficit. But just as the gains from the economic growth had gone disproportionately to a small number, the gains from the recovery went disproportionately to a small number. Firms gave out options at low share prices when the stock market was weak, which allowed executives to clean up in a market that owed its recovery to the bailout and stimulus. On the day the Reconnecting to Work conference began, *USA Today* reported that CEO pay had jumped 27 percent in 2010 under the headline "CEO Pay Soars While Workers' Pay Stalls" (Kantz and Hansen 2011).[3]

But while executive pay and corporate profits recovered smartly, there was virtually no recovery in the job market. And the recession-induced deficits in the public sector produced cutbacks in government employment and spending with threats of more to come.

## The Resilience of the Grinches

*How the Grinch Stole Christmas* ends when the Whos overcome their disappointment at the stolen Christmas stockings, presents, and cookies, and join hands to celebrate Christmas because Christmas meant more to them than material goods bought in a store. This behavior shocked the Grinch to a born-again moment. Seuss reports the event: " . . . in Who-ville they say, That the Grinch's small heart grew three sizes that day."

Given the physiological problems of tripling even a small interior organ, note that Seuss does not himself claim this is what happened. He just reports what folks in Who-ville say. In any case, caught up with the Christmas spirit, the Grinch returned the stolen goods to the community. Then, to the surprise of all, "He himself . . . The Grinch carved up the roast beast" for Christmas dinner.

This is where Seuss and economic reality part. No one, least of all an economist, expects Americans to take the loss of prosperity and full employment in the Christmas spirit of the Whos, holding hands and singing. Unemployment reduces happiness, creates mental distress, worsens lifetime career prospects, and reduces family income, leading some into poverty.[4] Surveys show that the vast majority of Americans have a dim view of the direction in which the country is heading: less than 25 percent believe that their children will do better economically than they do (Bendavid 2011; Rasmussen Reports 2011).

Similarly, no one, least of all an economist, expected the Wall Street Grinches to have a spiritual rebirth and return their bailout-created gains to the country. But given the near-death experience of finance, I anticipated some change in behavior: apologies for what Wall Street had done to the country, thanks to taxpayers for bailing them out, and special thanks to the Obama administration for not siccing the FDIC and FBI onto them, as Presidents Reagan and Bush had done to the bankers who created the 1980s savings and loan crisis, and as New Deal investigators had done to their predecessors in the Great Depression. Given that even conservative Americans harbored distrust and anger toward the bankers, it seemed a good time for them to lay low, take a modest million or two in pay, donate to philanthropic causes, and maybe even volunteer to help the nation rebuild shared prosperity for all.

Instead, the Grinches of finance behaved just as the economists' model of homo oeconimicus predicts people behave when money is at stake. Evincing neither remorse nor interest in any interest but their own, Wall Street financiers fought to restore the past economic order in which they and their compatriots in the upper income brackets garnered all the gains from economic growth. A consumer financial protection agency to protect citizens in financial transactions? A Tobin tax on financial transactions? The Volcker rule? Higher capital requirements on banks? A policy to break up the banks too big to fail? Strengthened regulatory powers for the Securities Exchange Commission? Tax increases on the wealthy? "Nevermore," quoth the Grinch—or was that the Raven? Increased unionization to protect the interests of the middle class? Unions? "Forget them." The middle class? "Charge them debit card fees, the dumb marks."

After the conference, I worried that *How the Grinch Stole Christmas* had too rosy an ending to represent the U.S. economy. The Grinch looked like a Wall Street operator, but his born-again soft spot would have made Gordon Gekko and his cronies cackle. After all, "Greed is right, greed works. Greed clarifies, cuts through, and captures the essence of the evolutionary spirit."[5] Perhaps I needed a tougher vision of the grinches of the world than Dr. Seuss offered.

Fourteen years after he published the *Grinch*, Dr. Seuss developed that tougher vision in *The Lorax* (1971). This is the only Seuss book that puts economic behavior at the heart of the story. It is a dark, grim tale of how the entrepreneurial Once-ler found a way to turn Truffula trees into Thneeds, "which everyone, EVERYONE, EVERYONE needs!" Crazy with greed, the Once-ler pushed production to the point where it destroyed the environment, destroyed every Truffula tree, turned the land into a horrific rustbelt of empty factories and buildings fallen apart, with "no more work to be done." Sadly, the book displays only the Once-ler's green hands and beady eyes, so whether the Once-ler looks more like Gordon Gekko or Mr. Madoff or—name your favorite or least favorite Wall Street banker—I do not know. My guess is that the Once-ler is in the Grinch family, but I could be wrong.

I did a Google search to find out more about the Grinch after his Christmas epiphany. The slithery sneering creature starred in a 1977 TV show called *Halloween Is Grinch Night*. Here Seuss painted a harsher character whose sole goal was to terrorize the Whos on Halloween by releasing his bag of horrors onto Who-ville. The only thing that stopped the Grinch was a brave, bespectacled little Who, who delayed the Grinch until past the witching hour. At the show's end the Grinch threatens to come back the next Halloween to do his evil work. In the Hollywood remake of the show, I envision Brooksley Born, the head of the Commodity Futures Trading Commission under President Clinton, playing the brave little Who. Born wanted to regulate the risky derivatives market, a move for which she was viciously attacked by Bob Rubin, Alan Greenspan, Larry Summers, and Arthur Levitt, and forced to resign from her job. As for the bag of horrors, we all know what it contains: more and more dangerous derivatives, credit default swaps, mortgage-backed securities. If the Christmas Grinch is too soft for you, think of Once-ler or the Grinch of Halloween.

## THE WAY FORWARD: HORTONOMICS

There is another side to the economics of Dr. Seuss—a positive message that economists of every political stripe find particularly appealing. This is the story of investment in *Horton Hatches the Egg* (1940). Recall, if you will, the situation. Mayzie, a lazy bird, has laid an egg and wants someone to replace her atop the nest so she can have a "short" holiday. She inveigles Horton to sit on the egg—not an easy task for a huge elephant—but he fixes the tree branch to hold him until Mayzie returns. Horton sits on the egg through summer, autumn, winter, and spring, and all the while, Mayzie does not appear. Seuss reports that she was partying in Palm Beach, but I heard that she was actually on the Cayman Islands with the corporate Grinches who find the tax haven more profitable than building job-creating businesses. If only we had her Tweets to resolve the issue. In any case, Horton kept sitting on the egg, repeating the motif that we all know so well. "I meant what I said, and I said what I meant . . . An elephant's faithful—one hundred percent."

Hunters capture Horton and sell him, the tree, and the egg to a circus, which sees money-making potential in an elephant hatching an egg in a tree. It charges 10 cents a peek. When the egg hatches, Mayzie suddenly appears and tries to foreclose the property: "It's MY egg!" she sputters. "You stole it from me. Get off of my nest and out of my tree." But when the egg pops, out comes "something brand new"—an elephant-bird with elephant ears, tail, and trunk and wings, who stays with Horton.

*Horton Hatches the Egg* has two messages for understanding our current economic situation. The first is that economic growth requires long-term investments—sitting on the egg. Investment in infrastructure, in R&D, in new plants and equipment, in risky innovations, and, in the case of the egg, the investment in human capital. Economic growth is harmed by short-term investments based on balloon loans or financial manipulations. The second message is that trust is important in a well-functioning economy. "I meant what I said, and I said what I meant." Sellers of securities who are faithful to their clients instead of betting against them. Management and employees who work cooperatively knowing that they will divide the resultant profits. Consumers who know that when they pay their debts, the bank will apply their payments to the debt with the highest interest rate.

In the tradition of attaching names to economic policies—the New Deal, the Fair Deal, Reaganomics, Clintonomics—I propose that policies to reverse the trend in inequality and restore full employment be labeled Hortonomics. I offer one specific policy that would fit the Horton label. This is to modify the corporate tax code so that firms cannot deduct as a cost of business huge payments to top executives in the form of pay for performance unless the incentive plan covers all workers.[6] Currently firms cannot deduct health and retirement plans as costs of business unless the plans cover all workers, so this modification would extend that practice to incentive pay plans. The proposal would increase the proportion of American workers covered by incentive pay. The workers would benefit from their firms' economic performance to a greater extent than now, which would motivate them to produce more.

During the Great Recession, firms in most OECD countries adapted work-sharing policies that traded lower productivity to save jobs while firms in the United States did the opposite, shedding workers so rapidly that productivity increased at record levels (Bureau of Labor Statistics

2011). In developing countries also, policies were shifting in favor of workers. Brazil and other Latin American countries raised minimum wages, used tax monies from the wealthy to fund education and transfer programs for the poor, and experienced both falling inequality and increased economic growth. Perhaps most telling, China adopted a policy of strengthening unions and labor laws to fight inequality.

But while Hortonomics had traction in other countries, it seemed outside U.S. political discourse, which was focused on cutting the federal deficit, and where many viewed discussion of inequality as raising a red banner of class warfare. The Whos in the United States who suffered from stagnant real earnings and unemployment seemed invisible in debates over economic policy. In April I could not see what would change the situation.

## And Then . . . the American Whos Speak

They spoke up first in New York City on September 17, 2011, when the Occupy Wall Street protestors sat down in Zuccotti Park around Wall Street under banners that read "We are the 99 percent." The protestors targeted economic inequality, corporate greed and corruption, and the dominance of Wall Street over the government as the main problems that troubled them. But they offered no explicit political or policy agenda and were suspicious of both Democrats and Republicans. The New York event set off similar protests in other U.S. cities and communities and spread to other parts of the world.

It is unclear how much staying power the occupiers have or whether their protests will influence policy. Unions, environmentalists, and many others on the left support them. Many leaders, from the president of the United States to the mayor of New York to the head of the Federal Reserve, expressed sympathy for and recognition of the validity of their concerns. Republican politicians have been more critical of the occupiers and defensive of Wall Street. At the minimum the occupiers have brought the rise in inequality and joblessness to the forefront of national discourse.

The 1954 book *Horton Hears a Who!* offers Seussian insight into what happens when Whos speak up and others hear their voice. The book begins "on the fifteenth of May" (in the big scheme of things, just a smidgeon away from the occupiers' first protest on September

17). Horton is taking a bath when he hears a small noise from a speck of dust in the air. His elephant ears allow him to hear the voices of the Whos even though he cannot see them. The smaller-eared denizens of the jungle mock Horton for hearing voices until the mayor of Who-ville gets every Who "to make noises in greater amounts." Crying out as a group, "Their voices were heard! They rang out loud and clear." Horton and the other animals then join to protect the Whos because "a person's a person, no matter how small."

Now that the Whos in this country have spoken and some leaders have begun to listen to their concerns, I am more optimistic than I was at the Reconnecting to Work conference that the United States will come out of Wall Street's financial implosion and the Great Recession with reforms that will restore full employment and prosperity for all citizens. I hope that economics and social science and, more broadly, policy analysis, are up to the task of developing efficient programs to help attain this goal.

## Notes

1. For data on inequality, see the Gini coefficients from the Central Intelligence Agency and the United Nations: http://en.wikipedia.org/wiki/List_of_countries _by_income_equality (accessed June 5, 2012). For data on social mobility, see OECD (2010, Chapter 5).
2. These data are from Piketty and Saez (2003). The figures for 2008 show a small drop in the share of the upper 0.1 percent due to the collapse of the stock market. I use 2007 data as likely to be more representative of the situation after the market recovered. There are only modest differences in the shares between 2007 and 2008.
3. An updated and lengthier analysis is available at http://www.usatoday.com/ money/companies/management/story/CEO-pay-2010/45634384/1 (accessed June 5, 2012).
4. See Chapters 2 and 4 in this volume. In Chapter 4 of the 2008 *Employment Outlook*, the OECD documents the deleterious effects of unemployment on mental health using panel data for several countries. Sullivan and von Wachter (2009) show that job displacement of blue-collar males increases mortality by 50 percent to 100 percent. Studies of college graduates (Kahn 2010; Oreopoulos, von Wachter, and Heisz 2006) show that a cohort that graduates in a recession suffers lower income for the bulk of its working life. Finally, Gallup polls show that the proportion of unemployed Americans diagnosed with depression is twice as high as the proportion of fully employed persons, and rises with the length of unemployment. http://www.gallup.com/poll/139604/worry-sadness-stress-increase -length-unemployment.aspx (accessed June 5, 2012).

5. IMDb's page for *Wall Street*, http://www.imdb.com/title/tt0094291/quotes (accessed June 5, 2012).
6. For the details of this plan see www.americanprogress.org/issues/2011/03/worker _productivity.html (accessed June 5, 2012).

## References

Bakija, Jon, Adam Cole, and Bradley T. Heim. 2010. *Jobs and Income Growth on Top Earners and the Causes of Changing Income Inequality: Evidence from U.S. Tax Return Data.* Department of Economics Working Paper No. 2010-24. Williamstown, MA: Williams College. http://web.williams.edu/ Economics/wp/BakijaColeHeimJobsIncomeGrowthTopEarners.pdf (accessed November 8, 2011).

Bendavid, Naftali. 2011. "Country Is Headed in Wrong Direction, 74% Say." *Wall Street Journal.* http://online.wsj.com/article/SB100014240529702047 7460457662718045 6112672.html (accessed November 8, 2011).

Bureau of Labor Statistics. 2011. *International Comparisons of Manufacturing Productivity and Unit Labor Cost Trends, 2010.* News release. Washington, DC: Bureau of Labor Statistics. http://www.bls.gov/news.release/pdf/ prod4.pdf (accessed November 8, 2011).

Freeman, Richard, Joseph Blasi, and Douglas Kruse. 2011. *Inclusive Capitalism for the American Workforce: Reaping the Rewards of Economic Growth through Broad-Based Employee Ownership and Profit Sharing.* Washington, DC: Center for American Progress. http://www.americanprogress .org/2011/03/workerproductivity.html (accessed November 8, 2011).

Kahn, Lisa B. 2010. "The Long-Term Labor Market Consequences of Graduating from College in a Bad Economy." *Labour Economics* 17(2): 303–316.

Kantz, Matt, and Barbara Hansen. 2011. "CEO Pay Soars While Workers' Pay Stalls." *USA Today*, April 1, 1:B. http://www.usatoday.com/money/ companies/management/story/CEO-pay-2010/45634384/1 (accessed November 8, 2011).

Marlar, Jenny. 2010. *Worry, Sadness, Stress Increase with Length of Unemployment: Majority of Unemployed are "Struggling."* Washington, DC: Gallup. http://www.gallup.com/poll/139604/worry-sadness-stress-increase-length-unemployment.aspx (accessed November 8, 2011).

Matai, D. K. 2009. *The Invisible One Quadrillion Dollar Equation.* Montreal: Globalresearch.ca. http://www.globalresearch.ca/index.php?context =va&aid=12753 (accessed November 8, 2011).

Mi2g. 2009. G20 *Summit Must Focus on Derivatives, Off-Balance-Sheet Vehicles: 8 Bubbles Quadrillion Play Grows 22 Percent to $206K per Person-on-Planet.* London: mi2g. http://www.mi2g.com/cgi/mi2g/frameset

.php?pageid=http%3A//www.mi2g.com/cgi/mi2g/press/190309.php (accessed November 8, 2011).

Oreopoulos, Philip, Till von Wachter, and Andrew Heisz. 2006. "The Short- and Long-Term Career Effects of Graduating in a Recession: Hysteresis and Heterogeneity in the Market for College Graduates." NBER Working Paper No. 12159. Cambridge, MA: National Bureau of Economic Research.

Organisation for Economic Co-operation and Development. 2008. *OECD Employment Outlook*. Paris: OECD.

———. 2010. "Economic Policy Reforms: Going for Growth." Paris: OECD. http://www.oecd.org/document/51/0,3343,en_2649_34325_44566259_1_1_1_1,00.html (accessed November 8, 2011).

Piketty, Thomas, and Emmanuel Saez. 2003. "Income Inequality in the United States, 1913–1998." *Quarterly Journal of Economics* 118(1): 1–39. (Tables and Figures Updated to 2008 in Excel format, July 2010).

Rasmussen Reports. 2011. *21% Say Today's Children Will Be Better Off Than Their Parents*. http://www.rasmussenreports.com/public_content/politics/general_politics/march_2011/21_say_today_s_children_will_be_better_off_than_their_parents (accessed November 8, 2011).

Seuss. 1940. *Horton Hatches the Egg*. New York: Random House.

———. 1954. *Horton Hears a Who!* New York: Random House.

———. 1957a. *The Cat in the Hat*. New York: Random House.

———. 1957b. *How the Grinch Stole Christmas*. New York: Random House.

———. 1971. *The Lorax*. New York: Random House.

Sullivan, Daniel, and Till von Wachter. 2009. "Job Displacement and Mortality: An Analysis Using Administrative Data." *Quarterly Journal of Economics* 124(3): 1265–1306.

U.S. Census Bureau. 2011. *Families*. Washington, DC: U.S. Census Bureau. http://www.census.gov/hhes/www/income/data/historical/families/index.html (accessed November 8, 2011).

# 1
# Introduction

Lauren D. Appelbaum
*Institute for Research on Labor and Employment*
*University of California–Los Angeles*

The Great Recession, the worst economic downturn since the Great Depression, was like none other in most of our lifetimes. No other recession in recent history has had comparable job losses. The second-worst recession, in 1981–1982, saw a drop of 2.8 million jobs, or 3.1 percent of payroll employment. By comparison, job losses from the Great Recession reached 7.9 million jobs, or 5.7 percent of payroll employment from December 2007 until jobs started to consistently increase in October 2010. As recently as February 2012, an additional 8.1 million people found themselves in part-time jobs when they actually wanted to be working full time, either because their hours had been cut or because there were no full-time positions available. At the recession's peak, the unemployment rate in the country was 10 percent, and over 26 million people were either unemployed, working part time for economic reasons, wanted a job but stopped looking because of personal reasons (e.g., school or family responsibility), or had become too discouraged to continue searching for a job (Bureau of Labor Statistics 2012a,b,c).

After nearly two years of recession, the U.S. economy entered a period of slow recovery in the third quarter of 2009. However, despite 11 quarters of gross domestic product (GDP) growth, jobs have just barely started to recover. Job growth was not consistent until October 2010, 16 months after the official end of the recession. Even after this point, job growth remained tepid, and the average job growth for the six months prior to and including February 2012 was still only about 200,000 jobs per month. At this rate, it will take more than eight years—until the end of 2020—to recover the jobs lost since the start of the recession and the approximately 100,000 jobs that should have been gained each month to account for the growth in the working-age population. Even if jobs continue to grow at the rate of almost 245,000 jobs per month that the country has experienced over the past three months (at the time of this writing, December 2011 to February 2012), it will take six years to get back to prerecession jobs levels (Bureau of Labor Statistics 2011a).

Furthermore, real GDP, which grew at a rate of 3 percent in 2010, slowed in 2011, and grew at an annual rate of 1.7 percent in 2011, according to the Bureau of Economic Analysis (2012). In order to make a dent in the jobs deficit and to decrease the unemployment rate, the economy needs to gain about 300,000 jobs each month, and GDP needs to grow at a rate of 5–6 percent annually until the labor market recovers. As a result of the anemic job growth experienced since the official end of the recession, the unemployment rate in the United States, which has fallen from 9.1 percent in August 2011 to 8.3 percent in January 2012 (and remained as of February 2012), is expected to stay above 8 percent for all of 2012 and 2013 (Bureau of Labor Statistics 2011b; Congressional Budget Office 2012). In February 2012, 12.8 million people still remained unemployed, 2.6 million were only marginally attached to the labor force, and as noted above, 8.1 million people were working part time for economic reasons (Bureau of Labor Statistics 2011c).[1]

Most notably, long-term unemployment in the United States has become a significant problem. As of February 2012, among the officially unemployed, 5.4 million, or 42.6 percent, had been out of work for more than six months, and 29.2 percent had been unemployed for a year or more; the average time to find a job had reached more than nine months (Bureau of Labor Statistics 2011c,d).[2] Furthermore, by February of 2012, the working-age population of the United States had grown by about 9.3 million people from the start of the recession, but the labor force had only grown by less than 1 million (Bureau of Labor Statistics 2011b). Since the labor force usually grows with the increase in the working-age population, this is a remarkable development. Certainly, some jobless people are looking at the poor economic climate and choosing not to enter the labor force, deciding instead, for example, to return to or stay in school. However, there are doubtless many others who—having had no luck in finding a job for six months, a year, or two years or more—have simply given up and left the labor force. This exodus of working-age people from the labor force suggests that the current unemployment rate understates the extent of joblessness, and as many of these discouraged workers reenter the labor force, the unemployment rate may remain high for some time to come, even as jobs continue to be created.

Extended periods of high joblessness have detrimental economic and financial impacts on workers and the economy that continue long after jobs have recovered. Such economic scarring has been demonstrated in previous recessions and is bound to be more severe and longer-lasting now, as a result of the Great Recession, given the nearly unprecedented levels of unemployment, underemployment, and long-term unemployment facing workers in the United States (Irons 2009). Indeed, a recent study of people who lost a job between 2008 and 2009 finds that only 7 percent had recovered or surpassed their previous financial status and maintained their lifestyle. Over one-third (36 percent) of survey respondents were classified as currently being devastated or wrecked. That is, they were either in fair or poor financial shape and believed that their lifestyle had faced a major change. Twenty-one percent of respondents believed that this major change in their lifestyle was permanent (Zukin, Van Horn, and Stone 2011).

Several areas that are negatively affected during recessions, particularly education, opportunity, and poverty, influence the extent to which an economic downturn will have a long-term economic effect. Unemployment can lead to decreased educational achievement among both children and adults. Children in families with an unemployed or underemployed parent may be faced with poor nutrition and the loss of a supportive learning environment. These children are less likely to excel in school. Young adults as well as returning students are struggling to achieve their educational goals because of reduced family incomes due to unemployment and underemployment. Since children and their parents have highly correlated levels of educational attainment, the abandonment of educational goals among young adults today is likely to have a negative impact on their children's education levels in the future. This loss in educational achievement is likely to continue to negatively impact the economy, as wages increase with educational success (Hertz et al. 2007; Irons 2009).

Researchers have found that people entering the workforce during an economic downturn fare worse than do workers who enter the workforce when the economy is healthy. As the unemployment rate rises, the impact on wages also increases. One study found a decrease in wages of 6–7 percent for each percentage-point increase in the unemployment rate at the time of entry into the workforce. For workers who have not graduated from college, the extent to which unemployment depresses wages is even more severe. In addition, these effects are long term, lasting as many as 15–20 years (Kahn 2010; von Wachter, Song, and Manchester 2007).

Furthermore, lower wages result in fewer opportunities and decreased economic success, not only for the workers themselves, but also for their children. Research has found that while we would expect job loss to result in reduced family incomes in the present, this decline in wages is surprisingly passed down to the next generation. The children of male job losers earn 9 percent less than their peers whose fathers did not lose a job (Oreopoulos, Page, and Stevens 2005). Given the millions of people who have lost a job during the recent economic downturn and continuing jobs crisis, wages and family incomes are likely to remain depressed for decades.

Not surprisingly, the current poverty rate in the United States is higher than it has been in nearly 30 years. At 15.1 percent in 2010, the poverty rate was just below its 1982 peak of 15.2 percent. Furthermore, the poverty rate is generally recognized as an outdated measure of poverty. In 2010, over one-third of Americans had an income that was below 200 percent of the poverty line, which is generally recognized as what it actually takes to get by (Fremstad 2011). Poverty in childhood has been correlated with future problems, such as criminal activity, poor health, and low earnings. Thus, the increase in poverty in the United States following the economic crisis is likely to be a drain on the economy into the next generation (Irons 2009).

These effects of unemployment do not tell the whole story, however. A substantial number of studies have found that unemployment has a negative effect on a large number of outcomes ranging from the physical to the social to the psychological. Decades of research have demonstrated a relationship between unemployment and poor overall health, increases in deaths due to cardiovascular problems, cirrhosis, and suicide, decreases in well-being, increases in depression, anxiety, and mental hospital admissions, and increases in alcohol abuse, violence, and arrests. A Rutgers University survey fielded in the summer of 2009 found that about two-thirds of unemployed respondents felt anxious, helpless, or depressed, and over three-quarters felt stressed. Furthermore, the length of unemployment makes a difference—a study of both blue- and white-collar workers found that psychological symptoms were greater after four months of unemployment than after one month (Blakely, Collings, and Atkinson 2003; Brenner 1967, 1979; Burgard, Brand, and House 2007; Catalano 1991; Catalano et al. 1993a,b; Catalano, Novaco, and McConnell 1997, 2002; Dooley, Catalano, and Rook 1988; Dooley, Catalano, and Wilson 1994; Dooley, Fielding, and Levi 1996; Eliason and Storrie 2009; Hagen 1983; Hamalainen et al. 2005; Iversen and Sabroe 1988; Kessler, Turner, and House 1988, 1989; Kposowa 2001; Liem and Liem 1988; Liem and Rayman 1982; Linn, Sandifer, and Stein 1985; Payne, Warr, and Hartley 1984; Rutgers University 2009; Smart 1979; von Wachter 2010; Warr, Jackson, and Banks 1988).

One outcome of the psychological trauma caused by living in a world of economic uncertainty is the impact it has on the decisions we make. For instance, researchers have shown a connection between job loss and marital and family dissolution. While marriage can help to soften the blow of unemployment, unemployment can lead to marital dissatisfaction. When one loses a job, one suffers not only financial hardship, but also a loss of identity and social networks. These losses may create difficulties in personal relationships. This strain may result in decisions to dissolve marriages or postpone getting married. Recent anecdotal evidence supports this research. Polls indicate an increase in the dissatisfaction among married couples and a decrease in the number of marriages in areas particularly hard hit by the recession (Grant and Barling 1994; Liem and Liem 1988; McKee-Ryan et al. 2005; Nasser and Overberg 2011; Peck 2010; Price, Friedland, and Vinokur 1998; Shrieves 2010; Wilcox 2009).

Unemployment creates insecurity and the disruption of plans, both current and future. Unemployment may also lead to limited finances, which may constrain personal choices. Furthermore, the time frame for reaching goals and milestones, such as buying a home, continuing on in education, becoming financially independent from one's parents, or beginning retirement, may be altered by poor economic conditions. There is some evidence that disruptive economic events during the life course can have consequences reaching well into the future (George 1993; Moen 1983; von Wachter, Song, and Manchester 2007).

Polls indicate a recent increase in college applications, but also suggest that people working their way through college have had to leave school. There has been a decline in the United States in both the fertility and birth rates since the start of the recession. The number of births in the United States fell by 2.6 percent in 2009, at the height of job loss, despite an increase in the population. We have witnessed an increase of female workers between 30 and 34 years of age since the start of the recession. These women may be delaying having children and thus staying in the workforce. In a 2009 survey, almost half of low- and middle-income women indicated that they planned to delay pregnancy or reduce the number of children they plan to have. Almost two-thirds of those surveyed said they could not affort to have a baby (Guttmacher Institute 2009; Hamilton, Martin, and Ventura 2010; Norris 2011; Tejada-Vera and Sutton 2010).

The growth in labor force participation since December 2007 among men between the ages of 62 and 64, as well as those above age 65, indicates that people may be delaying retirement and working longer. Furthermore, there was a 7.6 percent increase in the number of people over 55 with jobs during the three years from the start of the recession in December 2007 to December 2010 and an associated rise in the unemployment rate for this group. And, when asked about retirement, nearly a quarter of the people participating in the 2010 Retirement Confidence Survey indicated that the age at which they plan to retire increased over the previous year (Arenson 2008; Foderaro 2009a,b; Employee Benefit Research Institute 2010; Norris 2011; Public Agenda 2009; Scheiber 2009; Sok 2010).

The decisions made not only by the unemployed but also by employed workers facing a difficult job market affect the workers themselves, as well as their families and communities. They could have serious implications for the future health of the U.S. economy, even decades beyond the end of the recession. Given the multitude of negative outcomes of job loss, the United States must find a way to recover from the current jobs crisis. It is important to understand both the economic and psychological outcomes of this crisis in order to have a more robust response that goes beyond economic stimulus and financial markets reform to address the lingering social and psychological impacts of prolonged weakness in the labor market.

In the context of the Great Recession and its aftermath, in April 2011 the Institute for Research on Labor and Employment at the University of California, Los Angeles, held a conference called Reconnecting to Work. Researchers, advocates, and practitioners from across the United States, Canada, and Europe came to Los Angeles to participate in the conference. The goal of the conference was to enable a better understanding of the consequences of long-term unemployment and the policies that are needed to address it. Speakers presented research that examined the psychological and economic consequences of experiencing a prolonged spell of joblessness. Discussion of policies to increase job creation and get the long-term unemployed back into jobs engaged both researchers and practitioners, and drew lively responses from the audience.

Presentations focused on what it means to be out of work for long periods, and the consequences, both economic and psychological, of this experience. One of the more unusual presentations examined responses of employers to the recession and high unemployment. Speakers discussed policy options for adjusting to declines in demand, including reducing hours of work rather than laying off workers. Speakers from Europe and the United States addressed these issues both from a national and international comparative perspective.

Several major themes arose from the conference presentations and are represented in the chapters in this volume. One recurring theme is that losses experienced as a result of unemployment will be felt for years. Economic losses persist for up to two decades, with measurable negative effects on the health of unemployed individuals and their families. It is not only physical health that is impaired by long spells of unemployment—long-term unemployment causes psychological distress that is not easily overcome. On the policy front, many speakers identified short-time compensation, in which workers are not laid off in a downturn but instead their hours are reduced and they draw partial unemployment benefits for the lost hours, as a policy that has proven successful in keeping unemployment from rising. Countries that have used this approach for dealing with declines in demand have experienced smaller increases in unemployment in relation to the decline in GDP than occurred in countries where this policy was not widely utilized.

World-renowned economist Richard Freeman gave the keynote address at the Reconnecting to Work conference. His address focused on Wall Street's role in the jobs crisis and the policies needed to return to full employment. A more formal version of Freeman's keynote address forms the foreword to this volume. With this provocative presentation, Freeman sets the stage for the substantive chapters of this book. Drawing on the whimsical writings of Dr. Seuss, Freeman makes serious points about the nature of the jobs crisis in the United States and focuses attention on what must change in order to resolve the problems of extreme inequality and high and persistent joblessness.

Because policymakers failed early on to recognize the severity of the economic problems facing the country and to adopt macroeconomic policies adequate to address them, the United States has experienced a period of persistent and long-term unemployment. As noted by Till von Wachter in Chapter 2 of this book, losing a job has economic repercussions for workers that take 15–20 years to overcome. Von Wachter says that although there is variation in degree, these economic losses are felt by all unemployed workers regardless of demographic factors or industry. Furthermore, poor economic outcomes can lead to poor health outcomes, which can extend to workers' families. Von Wachter's chapter explores the negative impact of unemployment and policy options for relieving the economic costs of job loss.

In Chapter 3, John Schmitt addresses the question of whether steep declines in GDP inevitably lead to sharp increases in unemployment. He examines the role that various labor market institutions play in muting or transmitting demand shocks to jobs. He does this by comparing national labor market institutions in Denmark, which is noted for the flexibility of its labor market and its use of retraining and job search assistance to match unemployed workers with jobs, with those in Germany, which include a range of measures that facilitate adjustment by firms to demand shocks via changes in hours of work rather than changes in number of employees. Schmitt looks to the example of Germany as the road not taken and argues that the nature of labor market institutions may explain the varying experiences of different countries during the downturn. In particular, Schmitt argues that Denmark, which had the most successful labor market of the 2000s, lacked the ability to adequately respond to periods of slack demand. The German labor market on the other hand, which allowed for a great deal of flexibility in adjusting hours worked, was able to prevent a steep decrease in GDP from resulting in skyrocketing unemployment. Quite to the contrary, Germany's unemployment rate decreased during the economic crisis, despite a decrease in GDP greater than that of the United States.

Thus far, the United States has not followed the German example, and the sharp decline in GDP during the economic crisis led to a doubling of the unemployment rate from 5 percent in December 2007 to 10 percent in October of 2009. While dropping fairly consistently since October 2010, unemployment remains at 8.3 percent (at the time of this writing), despite more than two and a half years of economic recovery.

In Chapter 4, Timothy M. Diette, Arthur H. Goldsmith, Darrick Hamilton, and William Darity Jr. examine the psychological footprint of unemployment and demonstrate a causal link between unemployment and emotional well-being. Using a new method for identifying this causal link, these authors are able to estimate the impact of unemployment on emotional health. Diette and colleagues also explore the way in which particular social characteristics interact with the detrimental effects of experiencing a bout of unemployment. Their research points to differing impacts of long- and short-term unemployment. Understanding the relationship between psychological well-being and unemployment is critical, given the unprecedented length of time it currently takes the average unemployed person to find a job.

In view of the failure of job growth to recover in the United States, different approaches to labor market policies that may increase employment must be explored. The next three chapters of this volume look at varying options for encouraging firms to step up hiring and/or to reduce layoffs, either of which will result in net increases in jobs in the economy.

In Chapter 5, Hilbrand Oldenhuis and Louis Polstra argue that getting employers to cooperate with social service agencies is essential to improving the jobs outlook. They determine that different psychological factors are important in predicting whether the people making hiring decisions at small, medium, and large firms will cooperate with social service agencies. The authors argue that these factors must be taken into consideration when attempting to elicit cooperation between firms and social service agencies. Oldenhuis and Polstra conclude that getting firms to cooperate is important for reducing the unemployment rate now and for preventing long-term unemployment as time goes on.

With the German example in mind, two of the chapters examine the implementation of short-time compensation programs, such as work sharing—the shortening of workers' hours in order to create work and increase employment by decreasing layoffs (Baker 2011). Through work sharing, employers can save money and resources by reducing the hours of their current employees while avoiding the costs of hiring and training a new workforce later. Employees benefit by keeping their jobs and maintaining their skills while receiving a proportionate amount of their unemployment benefit for the time not worked, and the government spends little or no more than it currently does for unemployment benefits.

Chapters 6 and 7 in this volume demonstrate the importance of labor market institutions and the value of work sharing as a solution to the current jobs crisis. Vera Brusentsev and Wayne Vroman in Chapter 6 discuss the features of short-time compensation and examine its use in the United States thus far. They then compare the programs in the United States with short-time compensation programs in Canada, Germany, and Belgium. Brusentsev and Vroman conclude that the program needs to be expanded in the United States in order to have a meaningful impact, and they discuss a legislative proposal that could do just that.

In Chapter 7, Michele Tiraboschi and Silvia Spattini examine how different EU member states have responded to the economic crisis and the impact of different policy choices on the unemployment rate in these countries. The authors conclude that while there is no one best solution to reducing job loss during a recession, a short-time work arrangement is a necessary element for preventing job loss and holding down increases in unemployment. Finally, these authors note that there has been a convergence of systems; short-time work arrangements as well as active labor market policies (such as training) that are intended to facilitate reintegration of the unemployed into employment are being utilized in European countries to respond to the crisis.

Recent slow growth is not enough to lead to a significant increase in jobs and reduction in unemployment. The Congressional Budget Office (2012) considers the current natural rate of unemployment to be about 6 percent and estimates that it will take about five years for the unemployment rate to reach the natural rate of unemployment, dropping to an average of 5.7 percent in 2017. Thus, despite 11 quarters of GDP growth, the recovery is both tenuous and jobless.

While political leaders in Washington are unable to agree on how to stimulate the economy and create jobs, the authors in this volume present a fresh approach to understanding the nature and causes of the jobs crisis, the economic and psychological consequences of high and persistent unemployment, and the policy approaches that can begin to make a difference, even in the current fraught political environment.

## Notes

1. People who are marginally attached to the labor force are out of work and have stopped looking for work either because they are too discouraged or for personal reasons. However, they are available for work and would take a job if offered one.
2. While the percentage of the unemployed who have remained out of work for more than six months is seasonally adjusted, the percentage of the unemployed who have remained out of work for a year or more is not seasonally adjusted.

## References

Arenson, Karen W. 2008. "Applications to U.S. Colleges Are Breaking Records." *New York Times*, January 17, A:22. http://www.nytimes.com/2008/01/17/education/17admissions.html?scp=1&sq=arenson+applications&st=nyt (accessed September 27, 2011).

Baker, Dean. 2011. *Work Sharing: The Quick Route Back to Full Employment.* Washington, DC: Center for Economic and Policy Research.

Blakely, Tony A., Sunny C. D. Collings, and June Atkinson. 2003. "Unemployment and Suicide: Evidence for a Causal Association?" *Journal of Epidemiology and Community Health* 57(8): 594–600.

Brenner, M. Harvey. 1967. "Economic Change and Mental Hospitalization: New York State, 1910–1960." *Social Psychiatry and Psychiatric Epidemiology* 2(4): 180–188.

———. 1979. "Influence of the Social Environment on Psychology: The Historical Perspective." In *Stress and Mental Disorder*, James E. Barrett, ed. New York: Raven Press, pp. 161–177.

Bureau of Economic Analysis. 2012. "Gross Domestic Product: Fourth Quarter and Annual 2011 (Second Estimate)." News release, February 29. Washington, DC: Bureau of Economic Analysis. http://www.bea.gov/newsreleases/national/gdp/2012/pdf/gdp4q11_2nd.pdf (accessed March 5, 2012).

Bureau of Labor Statistics. 2012a. *Employment, Hours, and Earnings from the Current Employment Statistics Survey.* Washington, DC: Bureau of Labor Statistics. http://www.bls.gov/data/ (accessed March 19, 2012).

———. 2012b. *Labor Force Statistics from the Current Population Survey.* Washington, DC: Bureau of Labor Statistics. http://www.bls.gov/data/ (accessed March 19, 2012).

———. 2012c. *The Employment Situation—February 2012*. Economic news release, March 9. Washington, DC: Bureau of Labor Statistics. http://www.bls.gov/news.release/empsit.nr0.htm (accessed March 19, 2012).

———. 2011d. *Household Data Not Seasonally Adjusted A-35. Unemployed Total and Full-Time Workers by Duration of Unemployment*. Washington, DC: Bureau of Labor Statistics. http://www.bls.gov/web/empsit/cpseea35.pdf (accessed March 19, 2012).

Burgard, Sarah A., Jennie E. Brand, and James S. House. 2007. "Toward a Better Estimation of the Effect of Job Loss on Health." *Journal of Health and Social Behavior* 48(4): 369–384.

Catalano, Ralph. 1991. "The Health Effects of Economic Insecurity." *American Journal of Public Health* 81(9): 1148–1152.

Catalano, Ralph, David Dooley, Raymond W. Novaco, Richard Hough, and Georjeanna Wilson. 1993a. "Using ECA Survey Data to Examine the Effect of Job Layoffs on Violent Behavior." *Hospital and Community Psychiatry* 44(9): 874–879.

Catalano, Ralph, David Dooley, Georjeanna Wilson, and Richard Hough. 1993b. "Job Loss and Alcohol Abuse: A Test Using Data from the Epidemiologic Catchment Area Project." *Journal of Health and Social Behavior* 34(3): 215–225.

Catalano, Ralph, Raymond W. Novaco, and William McConnell. 1997. "A Model of the Net Effect of Job Loss on Violence." *Journal of Personality and Social Psychology* 72(6): 1440–1447.

———. 2002. "Layoffs and Violence Revisited." *Aggressive Behavior* 28(3): 233–247.

Congressional Budget Office (CBO). 2012. *The Budget and Economic Outlook: Fiscal Years 2012–2022*. Washington, DC: CBO. http://www.cbo.gov/sites/default/files/cbofiles/attachments/01-31-2012_Outlook.pdf (accessed March 19, 2012).

Dooley, David, Ralph Catalano, and Karen S. Rook. 1988. "Personal and Aggregate Unemployment and Psychological Symptoms." *Journal of Social Issues* 44(4): 107–123.

Dooley, David, Ralph Catalano, and Georjeanna Wilson. 1994. "Depression and Unemployment—Panel Findings From the Epidemiologic Catchment-Area Study." *American Journal of Community Psychology* 22(6): 745–765.

Dooley, David, Jonathan Fielding, and Lennart Levi. 1996. "Health and Unemployment." *Annual Review of Public Health* 17(1): 449–465.

Eliason, Marcus, and Donald Storrie. 2009. "Does Job Loss Shorten Life?" *Journal of Human Resources* 44(2): 277–302.

Employee Benefit Research Institute (EBRI). 2010. *How Many Workers Are Delaying Retirement? Why?* Fast Facts No. 162. Washington, DC: EBRI.

http://www.ebri.org/pdf/FFE162.28April10.RetDelay-RCS.Final.pdf (accessed September 27, 2011).

Foderaro, Lisa W. 2009a. "Two-Year Colleges, Swamped, No Longer Welcome All." *New York Times,* November 12, A:27. http://www.nytimes.com/2009/11/12/education/12community.html?scp=5&sq=Foderaro&st=nyt (accessed September 27, 2011).

————. 2009b. "Well-Regarded Public Colleges Get a Surge of Bargain Hunters." *New York Times*, March 2, A:1. http://www.nytimes.com/2009/03/02/nyregion/02suny.html?scp=10&sq=Foderaro&st=nyt (accessed September 27, 2011).

Fremstad, Shawn. 2011. "New Census Numbers Make It Official: 2000–2010 Was a Lost Economic Decade." Washington, DC: Center for Economic and Policy Research. http://www.cepr.net/index.php/data-bytes/poverty-bytes/new-census-numbers-make-it-official-2000-2010-was-lost-economic-decade (accessed September 26, 2011).

George, Linda K. 1993. "Sociological Perspectives on Life Transitions." *Annual Review of Sociology* 19(1): 353–373.

Grant, Sally, and Julian Barling. 1994. "Linking Unemployment Experiences, Depressive Symptoms, and Marital Functioning: A Meditational Model." In *Job Stress in a Changing Workforce: Investigating Gender Diversity*, Gwendolyn P. Keita, Joseph J. Hurrell Jr., eds. Washington, DC: American Psychological Association, pp. 311–327.

Guttmacher Institute. 2009. *A Real-Time Look at the Impact of the Recession on Women's Family Planning and Pregnancy Decisions*. Washington, DC: Guttmacher Institute. http://www.guttmacher.org/pubs/RecessionFP.pdf (accessed April 16, 2012).

Hagen, Duane Q. 1983. "The Relationship between Job Loss and Physical and Mental Illness." *Hospital and Community Psychiatry* 34(5): 438–441.

Hamalainen, Juha, Kari Poikolainen, Erkki Isometsa, Jaakko Kaprio, Martti Heikkinen, Sari Lindeman, and Hillevi Aro. 2005. "Major Depressive Episode Related to Long Unemployment and Frequent Alcohol Intoxication." *Nordic Journal of Psychiatry* 59(6): 486–491.

Hamilton, Brady E., Joyce A. Martin, Stephanie J. Ventura. 2010. "Births: Preliminary Data for 2009." *National Vital Statistics Reports* 59(3): 1–19. Washington, DC: Center for Disease Control (CDC). http://www.cdc.gov/nchs/data/nvsr/nvsr59/nvsr59_03.pdf (accessed September 27, 2011).

Hertz, Tom, Tamara Jayasundera, Patrizio Piraino, Sibel Selcuk, Nicole Smith, and Alina Verashchagina. 2007. "The Inheritance of Educational Inequality: International Comparisons and Fifty-Year Trends." *The B.E. Journal of Economic Analysis & Policy* 7(2): 1–46. http://www.bepress.com/cgi/

viewcontent.cgi?article=1775&context=bejeap (accessed September 26, 2011).

Irons, John. 2009. "Economic Scarring: The Long-Term Impacts of the Recession." EPI Briefing Paper No. 243. Washington, DC: Economic Policy Institute. http://www.epi.org/publication/bp243/ (accessed September 26, 2011).

Iversen, Lars, and Svend Sabroe. 1988. "Psychological Well-Being among Unemployed and Employed People after a Company Closedown: A Longitudinal Study." *Journal of Social Issues* 44(4): 141–152.

Kahn, Lisa B. 2010. "The Long-Term Labor Market Consequences of Graduating from College in a Bad Economy." *Labour Economics* 17(2): 303–316.

Kessler, Ronald C., J. Blake Turner, and James S. House. 1988. "Effects of Unemployment on Health in a Community Survey: Main, Modifying, and Mediating Effects." *Journal of Social Issues* 44(4): 69–85.

———. 1989. "Unemployment, Reemployment, and Emotional Functioning in a Community Sample." *American Sociological Review* 54(4): 648–657.

Kposowa, Augustine J. 2001. "Unemployment and Suicide: A Cohort Analysis of Social Factors Predicting Suicide in the U.S. National Longitudinal Mortality Study." *Psychological Medicine* 31(1): 127–138.

Liem, Ramsay, and Joan H. Liem. 1988. "Psychological Effects of Unemployment on Workers and Their Families." *Journal of Social Issues* 44(4): 87–105.

Liem, Ramsay, and Paula Rayman. 1982. "Health and Social Costs of Unemployment: Research and Policy Considerations." *American Psychologist* 37(10): 1116–1123.

Linn, Margaret W., Richard Sandifer, and Shayna Stein. 1985. "Effects of Unemployment on Mental and Physical Health." *American Journal of Public Health* 75(5): 502–506.

McKee-Ryan, Frances M., Zhaoli L. Song, Connie R. Wanberg, and Angelo J. Kinicki. 2005. "Psychological and Physical Well-Being during Unemployment: A Meta-Analytic Study." *Journal of Applied Psychology* 90(1): 53–76.

Moen, Phyllis. 1983. "Unemployment, Public Policy, and Families: Forecasts for the 1980s." *Journal of Marriage and Family* 45(4): 751–760.

Nasser, Haya El, and Paul Overberg. 2011. "Fewer Couples Embrace Marriage; More Live Together." *USA Today*, May 26. http://yourlife.usatoday.com/sex-relationships/marriage/story/2011/05/Marriage-loses-ground/47625450/yourlife.usatoday.com/?loc=interstitialskip (accessed November 10, 2011).

Norris, Floyd. 2011. "Older Workers Are Keeping a Tighter Grip on Jobs." *New York Times*, January 15, B:3. http://www.nytimes.com/2011/01/15/

business/15charts.html?_r=1&nl=afternoonupdate&emc=aua22 (accessed September 27, 2011).

Oreopoulos, Philip, Marianne Page, and Ann Huff Stevens. 2005. "The Inter-generational Effects of Worker Displacement." NBER Working Paper No. 11587. Cambridge, MA: National Bureau of Economic Research. http://www.nber.org/papers/w11587 (accessed September 27, 2011).

Payne, Roy, Peter Warr, and Jean Hartley. 1984. "Social Class and Psychological Ill-Health during Unemployment." *Sociology of Health & Illness* 6(2): 152–174.

Peck, Don. 2010. "How a New Jobless Era Will Transform America." *The Atlantic Online*, March. http://www.theatlantic.com/doc/201003/jobless-america-future (accessed September 27, 2011).

Price, Richard H., Daniel S. Friedland, and Anuram D. Vinokur. 1998. "Job Loss: Hard Times and Eroded Identity." In *Perspectives on Loss: A Sourcebook*, John H. Harvey, ed. Philadelphia, PA: Taylor & Francis, pp. 303–316.

Public Agenda. 2009. "National Survey Finds Work, Family Responsibilities Fueling Low College Completion Rates." December 9. New York: Public Agenda. http://www.publicagenda.org/press-releases/theirwholelivesaheadofthem (accessed September 27, 2011).

Rutgers University. 2009. *The Anguish of Unemployment: September 2009.* New Brunswick, NJ: John J. Heldrich Center for Workforce Development, Edward J. Bloustein School of planning and Public Policy, Rutgers University. http://www.heldrich.rutgers.edu/sites/default/files/content/Heldrich_Work_Trends_Anguish_Unemployment.pdf (accessed September 27, 2011).

Scheiber, Noam. 2009. "Retirement and the Recession, Cont'd." *The New Republic*, October 10. http://www.tnr.com/print/blog/the-stash/retirement-and-the-recession-contd (accessed September 27, 2011).

Shrieves, Linda. 2010. "The Marriage Recession: As Unemployment Rises, So Does the Divorce Rate." *Times-Picayune*, January 5.

Smart, Reginald G. 1979. "Drinking Problems among Employed, Unemployed and Shift Workers." *Journal of Occupational and Environmental Medicine* 21(11): 731–736.

Sok, Emy. 2010. "Record Unemployment among Older Workers Does Not Keep Them Out of the Job Market." *Issues in Labor Statistics: Summary 10-04*, March. Washington, DC: U.S. Bureau of Labor Statistics. http://data.bls.gov/cgi-bin/print.pl/opub/ils/summary_10_04/older_workers.htm (accessed September 27, 2011).

Tejada-Vera, Betzaida, and Paul D. Sutton. 2010. "Births, Marriages, Divorces, and Deaths: Provisional Data for October 2009." *National Vital*

*Statistics Reports* 58(25): 1–6. http://www.cdc.gov/nchs/data/nvsr/nvsr58/nvsr58_25.pdf (accessed April 16, 2012).

von Wachter, Till. 2010, April 29. *Long-Term Unemployment: Causes, Consequences and Solutions.* Testimony for the Joint Economic Committee, U.S. Congress. http://www.columbia.edu/~vw2112/testimony_JEC_vonWachter_29April2010.pdf (accessed September 27, 2011).

von Wachter, Till, Jae Song, and Joyce Manchester. 2007. "Long-Term Earnings Losses Due to Job Separation during the 1982 Recession: An Analysis Using Longitudinal Administrative Data from 1974 to 2004." Discussion Paper No. 0708-16. New York: Columbia University, Department of Economics.

Warr, Peter, Paul Jackson, and Michael Banks. 1988. "Unemployment and Mental Health: Some British Studies." *Journal of Social Issues* 44(4): 47–68.

Wilcox, W. Bradford. 2009, December 11. "Can the Recession Save Marriage?" *Wall Street Journal.* http://online.wsj.com/article/SB10001424052748703558004574584042851448128.html (accessed September 27, 2011).

Zukin, Cliff, Carl E. Van Horn, and Charley Stone. 2011. "Categorizing the Unemployed by the Impact of the Recession." John J. Heldrich Center for Workforce Development working paper. New Brunswick, NJ: John J. Heldrich Center for Workforce Development. http://www.heldrich.rutgers.edu/sites/default/files/content/Categorizing_Impact_Recession_Revised_0.pdf (accessed December 2, 2011).

# 2
# Job Displacements in Recessions

## An Overview of Long-Term
## Consequences and Policy Options

Till von Wachter
*University of California–Los Angeles*
*National Bureau of Economic Research,*
*Centre for Economic Policy Research,*
*Institute for the Study of Labor*

As the U.S. economy continues to recover from the Great Recession, an important unknown is the fate of the millions of workers affected by layoffs and lengthening spells of unemployment. This chapter focuses on the short- and long-term consequences of layoffs and unemployment for affected workers, and on potential policy options to ease the burden of adjustment on workers and their families.

Judging from experience in past recessions, the consequences of layoffs for job losers are severe and persistent across several dimensions. The average mature worker losing a stable job with a good employer will see earnings reductions of 20 percent lasting over 15–20 years. While these earnings losses vary somewhat among demographic groups or industries, no group in the labor market is exempt from significant and long-lasting costs of job loss (von Wachter, Song, and Manchester 2011a).

A job loss is also typically followed by an extended period of instability of employment and earnings. During this period, job losers can experience declines in health. In severe downturns, these health declines can lead to a significant reduction in life expectancy of 1–1.5 years (Sullivan and von Wachter 2009). The consequences of job loss are also felt by workers' children—who can suffer even into adulthood—and their families. All of these costs are likely to be greater for the long-term unemployed.

Government programs can alleviate part of the short-term earnings loss associated with job loss and unemployment. As a typical measure, extensions of unemployment insurance (UI)

- ease the burden of adjustment for laid-off workers,
- are likely to prevent entry into more costly government programs such as disability insurance,
- provide a degree of demand stabilization, and
- are unlikely—at least in recessions—to be associated with significant reductions in employment in the short or the long run.

However, policy is unlikely to be able to prevent the large and lasting reductions in earnings that eventually follow a typical job loss. The majority of long-term losses are due to factors that are not easily manipulated by government policy, such as losses in the value of certain skills as industries decline, the loss of long-term career jobs, or slow wage-adjustment in the labor market. Some policies, though, have been shown to be able to reduce unemployment, such as targeted efforts to help workers in their job search, or programs reducing the costs of long-term adjustment, such as the costs of retraining.

Given the difficulties of helping job losers and unemployed workers recover from long-term earnings losses after the fact, it may be worthwhile to explore available options to prevent large-scale layoffs in the future. Such options include programs of work sharing to subsidize employment before workers are laid off and become unemployed, to encourage the introduction of flexible work-time arrangements, or to encourage the provision of credit to economically viable firms affected by distress in financial markets.

For example, the cost of UI benefits for a typical worker is a small fraction of the total earnings lost due to a layoff over the remainder of the individual's working life. If the same benefits were paid during employment to avoid job loss, the cost of recessions would be substantially reduced. This would be beneficial even if the worker were to be let go eventually, since earnings losses tend to be significantly smaller for layoffs that do not occur in a large recession.

Overall, job loss and unemployment during severe recessions can impose substantial and lasting costs on affected workers in terms of earnings, health, and strain on their families. The short-term burden of these costs can in part be alleviated at a comparatively small cost, such as by extensions in UI. Less is known about how to help reduce the substantial long-term costs. While cost-effective policies may be available to help reemploy the long-term unemployed, the potential of policy interventions to significantly aid recovery of long-term earnings declines appears bleaker. Given these large and long-term costs, preventive measures to avoid massive layoffs are a policy option worth considering.

## THE SHORT- AND LONG-TERM CONSEQUENCES OF LAYOFF AND UNEMPLOYMENT

An increasing literature has documented that job losses during recessions have severe and lasting consequences for earnings. For example, workers displaced in the recession of the early 1980s—which, until 2008, was the strongest U.S. recession since World War II—on average had earnings reductions of 30 percent or more in the first year after layoff. These losses declined somewhat over time, but even 15–20 years after job loss, the earnings reduction was still 20 percent (Jacobson, Lalonde, and Sullivan 1993; von Wachter, Song, and Manchester 2011a). Such lasting earnings reductions occurred for job losers in all age ranges, in all industries, for men and women, and throughout the earnings distribution. This phenomenon is not limited to the early 1980s recession or to particular regions of the country, and it does not depend on the particular way of measuring the cost of displacement.[1] Older workers suffer larger losses in earnings, but these losses extend over shorter periods of time, since remaining lives are shorter and job loss hastens retirement (Chan and Stevens 2001). Workers in the middle of the education distribution, such as workers with some college or only a high school degree, appear to lose more than very low- or very high-skilled individuals (von Wachter and Handwerker 2009).

These long-lasting reductions in earnings occur alongside, and may be partly augmented by, increases in job instability, recurring transitions to nonemployment, and repeated switches of industry or occupation (Stevens 1997; von Wachter, Song, and Manchester 2011a). Some of this increased mobility between jobs may be a sign of beneficial adjustment, but on average those workers who immediately find a stable job in their predisplacement industry do significantly better. The increase in job instability lasts up to 10 years after layoff. During the same period, these workers experience continuing increases in earnings instability. Thus, there is no sign that laid-off workers trade lower earnings for more stable employment. While heightened regional mobility appears beneficial in the short run, as mobile workers may eschew a particularly depressed local labor market, movers do not have lower long-term earnings losses.

There is also increasing evidence that laid-off workers suffer short- and long-term declines in health. In the short term, layoffs and unemployment are associated with an increasing incidence of stress-related health problems, such as strokes or heart attacks (Burgard, Brand, and House 2007). These problems can lead to a large spike in mortality right after job loss. For example, mature men who lost their stable jobs in Pennsylvania during the early 1980s experienced an increase in the mortality rate right after job loss of up to 100 percent. This initial rise in mortality declines over time, but mortality remains significantly higher for job losers than for comparable workers who did not lose their jobs. If sustained until the end of their lives, such increases lead to reductions in life expectancy of 1–1.5 years (Sullivan and von Wachter 2009).

Several studies also point to short- and long-term effects of layoffs on the children and families of job losers and unemployed workers. For example, in the short run, parental job loss reduces schooling achievement of children (Stevens and Schaller 2009). In the long run, it appears that a lasting reduction in the earnings of fathers also reduces the earnings prospects of their sons (Oreopoulos, Page, and Stevens 2008). There is also evidence that layoff heightens the incidence of divorce, reduces home ownership, and increases the rate of application to and the receipt of disability insurance programs (Charles and Stephens 2004; Rege, Telle, and Votruba 2009; Rupp and Stapleton 1995; von Wachter and Handwerker 2009).

All of these costs are likely to be larger for workers who are unemployed for longer periods of time. It is well documented that earnings losses for unemployed workers increase significantly with time spent outside employment (Congressional Budget Office 2007; Machin and Manning 1999). It is difficult to establish whether this is because the duration itself worsens labor market prospects, or because those workers facing the strongest challenges in the labor market take longer to find a new job. In one of a few studies establishing causality, Schmieder, von Wachter, and Bender (2012b) show that nonemployment indeed leads to lower reemployment wages, at least in Germany. Independently of the source, longer unemployment spells are likely to put a significant additional strain on workers' financial situations and the overall well-being of both themselves and their families. These workers are also particularly dependent on benefits from UI. The poverty rate among the long-term unemployed is high, especially for those exhausting unemployment benefits (Congressional Budget Office 2008, Tables 6 and 9).

Finally, even though they were not laid off or are not officially counted as unemployed, the long-term earnings and career prospects of young workers entering the labor market during a recession also suffer. For example, individuals graduating from college during a large recession are likely to see reduced earnings for 10–15 years compared to more fortunate graduates (Kahn 2010; Oreopoulos, von Wachter, and Heisz 2012; Oyer 2008). As is the case for job losers, those labor market entrants in the middle of the education distribution do worse, while those with lower or higher education tend to do better (Kondo 2008; Oreopoulos, von Wachter, and Heisz 2012). The pattern of recovery of unlucky college graduates is telling: a recession reduces the quality of the first employer. After about five years, workers find an employer of better quality, but their earnings still have to recover within the firm relative to more fortunate graduates who obtained their jobs in better economic times. Thus, the initial setback in the career can take 10–15 years to dissipate, even for this very mobile demographic group.

## THE REASONS FOR LONG-TERM EARNINGS LOSSES AFTER LAYOFF AND UNEMPLOYMENT

There are several potential sources of lasting reductions in earnings after a layoff. An often cited explanation attributes the losses in earnings to a loss in the use of certain skills, as some industries or occupations shift their operations elsewhere or permanently reduce their employment levels. If some of workers' earnings derived from payment for services and skills only needed in specific industries or occupations, upon job loss workers lose wages associated with these skills (Neal 1995; Parent 2000; Poletaev and Robinson 2008). Such a loss can lead to long-term earnings declines if workers do not reinvest in a new equivalent set of skills. Particularly for middle-aged or older workers, it might not be worth spending their time and money in costly retraining as they face uncertain reemployment over a shorter remaining working life.

Another explanation is that workers in stable jobs, especially workers aged 30 or older, are likely to have found an occupation and an employer suitable for their interests and qualifications. The process of searching for such a job can take time, involving both changes of occupations and employers in the beginning of their careers, as well as job search and promotions within a firm (Baker, Gibbs, and Holmstrom 1994; Neal 1999; Topel and Ward 1992). On average, this phase of workers' careers can last 10 years. Part of the gain from this prolonged search and matching process is lost at job loss. By its nature, finding such a suitable job again is likely to take a long time. If job offers start arriving only as the economy picks up, the adjustment process can last well beyond recovery in the aggregate labor market.

Increasing evidence also suggests that the first wage on a worker's new job is likely to influence her pay for a long time (Beaudry and DiNardo 1991; Schmieder and von Wachter 2010). This persistence can arise from (explicit or implicit) wage contracts between workers and firms. Since many unemployed workers end up finding the first job when wages are still depressed due to the recession, persistence implies that they may live with lower earnings for quite some time. As a result, workers laid off in recessions suffer substantially larger earnings losses than workers laid off in booms (Davis and von Wachter 2012). Although workers can improve their pay by obtaining outside job offers, changing jobs, or relocating, many face obstacles to such adjustment, often due to family commitments. However, the rate of mobility is likely to be too low even given those factors, possibly because individuals do not realize the need to keep improving their economic situations 5–10 years after a job loss or an unemployment spell.

Some workers may also experience reductions in earnings because they held jobs in industries or at firms that paid exceptionally high wages. Yet, it does not appear that workers in such jobs are more likely to be laid off. In fact, during large recessions job losers are less likely to be selected from high-wage jobs, partly because economic difficulties are widespread and do not just affect single firms or sectors. Similarly, it is unlikely that job losses arise because firms systematically let go those workers who are overpaid or who are least productive.[2]

## POLICY OPTIONS TO EASE THE BURDEN OF ADJUSTMENT OF LAID-OFF AND UNEMPLOYED WORKERS

### Policies Aimed at Reducing the Burden of Short-Term Earnings Losses

Government programs can help to ease the burden of the short-term cost of job loss and unemployment. The most common approach to do so has been to increase the duration over which eligible workers can receive unemployment benefits. In the 2008 recession, the maximum duration of UI benefits was 99 weeks, about four times the regular duration of 26 weeks. Significant extensions in the duration of UI also took place in the 1982 and 1990 recessions (Congressional Budget Office 2004).

Extensions of UI benefits have several beneficial aspects for recipients and for the economy as a whole. Extended benefits allow workers to buffer the effect of the earnings loss on consumption, albeit consumption still falls for the average UI recipient (Browning and Crossley 2001; Congressional Budget Office 2007; Gruber 1997). In addition, extended benefits allow workers to search longer for a suitable job, and provide insurance against the stress of not being able to find a job because of continued slack in the labor market. Extensions in UI benefits also prevent some workers from applying to other government programs not intended to smooth short-term economic shocks, such as Social Security Disability Insurance or Old Age and Survivors Insurance. In particular, benefits provided under disability insurance can be very costly, especially if provided to younger or middle-aged workers with low-mortality impairment (Autor and Duggan 2006; von Wachter, Song, and Manchester 2011b). While increases in unemployment rates typically lead to a significant rise in application and award rates, extensions in UI have the potential to dampen this effect. Finally, extended

UI benefits can provide a degree of demand stabilization through the multiplier effect (Congressional Budget Office 2008, Table 1).

On the downside, several studies have suggested that UI may impose a cost by reducing recipients' willingness to work (Congressional Budget Office 2008).[3] In addition, prolonged spells of unemployment may lead workers' skills to atrophy or otherwise reduce their employability. Yet, it is likely that in severe recessions the benefit of extended UI outweighs the costs. First, the value of income replacement to workers should be particularly high. Second, longer UI durations are unlikely to have a strong effect on employment, since strategic considerations are likely to be weaker when the number of jobs is scarce (see, for example, Congressional Budget Office [2008]). Moreover, recent research suggests that a sizable part of the decline in employment may not be due to the reduction in the willingness of UI recipients to work, but rather to the fact that some individuals have limited access to credit. If this is the case, not all of the employment effects of UI represent a distortion, but it may be a sign that UI helps to alleviate credit constraints that prevent individuals from self-insuring against unemployment shocks.[4]

In the only study of its kind, Schmieder, von Wachter, and Bender (2012a) analyze large extensions in the durations of UI in Germany and show that these led to only moderate reductions in employment, without a noticeable difference in this effect in large recessions. Based on a very large sample of unemployed workers spanning over 25 years and utilizing a very credible research design, these findings lie at the lower range of typical U.S. estimates (Meyer 2002, Table 5). For a large increase in UI duration from 26 to 99 weeks, the estimates from Germany suggest that extended UI would lead to a moderate increase in the rate of unemployment. Yet, for several reasons the current effect in the United States would likely be smaller. The increases in UI durations were stepwise, and extension was not always certain. Only 50 percent of all eligible unemployed workers have taken up UI benefits in this recession, further reducing the potential impact of UI extensions on employment.[5] Finally, the effects on aggregate employment are based on the assumption of full employment; under a slack labor market, the effect of individual search decisions on aggregate employment is likely to be smaller.[6]

This research also suggests that contrary to what is often believed, extensions in UI benefits appear to neither help nor strongly hurt the longer-term job prospects of recipients. Increases in UI durations have small negative effects on the wage at the first job after unemployment. Yet, neither the wage nor the employment rate five years after entry into unemployment is affected by longer UI durations (Schmieder, von Wachter, and Bender 2012b). Thus, it appears that extended UI benefits have an effect on workers' disposable income, consumption, and short-term employment choice, but they may have neither strong adverse nor beneficial effects on long-term employment prospects.

Several other measures to ease the short-term burden of adjustment have been tried in the current and in past downturns, and have been featured in policy proposals in the 2008 recession. These include wage subsidies paid to employers and tax breaks for firms to raise job creation, temporary assistance to obtain further training, and some form of public employment. The best available evidence suggests that these measures are somewhat successful in reducing unemployment and alleviating earnings losses of job losers.[7] These measures do not share the advantage of extended UI, which builds on an existing infrastructure of a successfully functioning program and immediately affects UI recipients and the economy (Congressional Budget Office 2008, Table 1). However, with the exception of training, the measures share with extended UI the mainly short-term focus, with less known long-term benefits for laid-off and unemployed workers.

## Policies Aimed at Reducing Long-Term Unemployment and Lasting Earnings Losses

The reach of the large losses in earnings, increases in job instability, and reductions in health goes beyond the duration of extended UI benefits. In fact, since the losses persist well beyond 5 or 10 years, the majority of the lifetime loss in earnings occurs after eligibility for UI benefits has expired. Yet, few policy options are available to alleviate the long-run costs of job loss and unemployment.

For example, there is no current evidence that the longer duration of UI benefits improves the long-term earnings or employment trajectories of the unemployed (Schmieder, von Wachter, and Bender 2012b). Similarly, the evidence of efforts to successfully train laid-off workers in new skills is mixed, and there is little evidence available on the long-term effects of other programs.[8] By the nature of the mechanisms behind long-term earnings losses as explained above, it is unlikely that any policy will completely close or significantly reduce the long-term earnings gap—short of altering the market's mechanisms of wage setting, the trade-offs governing workers' investment in their skills, or the multiple factors affecting the decision to relocate. Yet, there are some options available to help those with long unemployment spells find jobs and try to improve the long-term earnings prospects of job losers.

In particular, it is likely that a lack in mobility between jobs, occupations, or regions will contribute to the persistence of reductions in earnings at job loss, perhaps because workers are not aware of the time it would take to dissipate their earnings losses. As explained above, the individual's recovery process is likely to last well beyond the recovery of the aggregate labor market. Job losers might not be aware of the long-term efforts required to rebuild a career, and active counseling may help in bringing expectations in line with the reality workers will be facing in the labor market. Evaluations of job search assistance have found that counseling reduces UI rolls and is cost-effective.[9]

Another reason why workers do not move or change occupations might be because they are not aware that the job prospects in their lines of work and in their local labor markets may have declined permanently. This may lead individuals to wrongly assess the prospects of finding a job in their old industries or occupations in their local labor markets, and wait too long to switch careers, change employers, or move to another region. Information on how job prospects in the workers' professions and related occupations are evolving both locally and nationally might be a useful tool to help unemployed workers and their families make better choices. Such information is routinely available from the Census Bureau and the Bureau of Labor Statistics, and could, for example, be included with workers' UI benefit checks.

Part of the effort to rebuild a career might involve retraining or relocating. One way to raise mobility is to offer workers support in covering expenses related to retraining or moving. Evaluations of subsidies to attend community college have found that they, on average, raise earnings of displaced workers, particularly if covered subjects are of a more technical nature. However, such programs seem to be beneficial and cost-effective for selected populations but may not be a solution for the broader population of participants (Jacobson, Lalonde, and Sullivan 2005). Less is known about the potential benefits of relocating unemployed workers. On the one hand, reallocation of labor across regions plays an important role in equilibrating local labor markets (Blanchard and Katz 1992). On the other hand, regional mobility does not appear to significantly lower earnings losses of displaced workers, perhaps because most large recessions afflict most regions of the country (von Wachter, Song, and Manchester 2011a). Yet, over the longer run, government programs helping unemployed workers to relocate, for example, by reducing their mortgage debt, are likely to help workers recover some of their lost earnings.

An alternative set of policies includes efforts to directly stimulate employment growth at the local level. These could be targeted at improving the economic situation in regions particularly hard hit by the recent downturn. Yet, in general, an upturn in the labor market improves the lot of some workers, but does not raise the earnings trajectory of job losers or those formerly unemployed (Jacobson, Lalonde, and Sullivan 1993; von Wachter, Song, and Manchester 2011a). There is no reason per se why localized policies should have a different effect on the employment of the long-term unemployed or the earnings of reemployed laid-off workers than a regular upturn in the labor market.

One reason why workers experiencing long-term unemployment spells are not affected by an improvement in labor market conditions is that they have become detached from the labor market. In this case, low-cost policies, such as informing workers about job opportunities or the employment outlook in their occupation, may not deliver the desired effect of increasing workers' mobility and raising their chances of finding a job. In this case, a more active approach may be needed to reintegrate long-term unemployed workers into the labor market. For example, it may be cost-efficient to temporarily subsidize workers' wages upon reemployment for a certain period if this leads to a permanent increase in labor force participation and reduces applications to programs geared for the disabled or the poor.[10]

Finally, given increasing evidence that children's long-term economic success might be influenced by the layoff of a parent, it is worth considering ways to directly assist families with children. One possibility that builds on existing programs is to provide additional financial aid to cover college tuition and living expenses. While work on the cross-generational effects of displacement is still developing, many families that experienced a layoff with children in college or nearing college age today are likely to feel the pinch in their financial resources. Thus, it may be worth exploring measures to help cover part of the costs of higher education or training for the children of job losers.

## Policy Initiatives to Avoid Mass Layoffs in Future Recessions

It is likely that cost-effective government policies can help the long-term unemployed find renewed employment. Yet, few measures promise to substantially reduce the long-term earnings losses that can afflict laid-off or unemployed workers. While Congress considers financial reform to safeguard against another financial crisis, it may be worth considering reforms that help prevent costly earnings losses during a future recession, such as work sharing. For jobs lost in declining firms or industries, this may mean that inevitable job destruction would be spread over time. Thus, layoffs would likely occur in a better economic environment and therefore lead to significantly smaller losses in earnings. For jobs lost in economically viable sectors or at viable firms, work sharing could avoid costly breakup of productive employment relationships that would have likely continued in the absence of an economic crisis.

Two mechanisms to achieve such a temporary buffering of employment at firms in economic difficulties could be work-sharing arrangements supported by the government, or private arrangements such as work-time accounts. Work sharing has effects that are similar to those of current measures to increase job creation through tax breaks or wage subsidies, except that incentives to generate employment are given prior to job displacement. In particular, instead of firing, say, 30 percent of its workers, an employer would reduce hours worked by all of its workers by 30 percent. Government subsidies comprise part of workers' reduced earnings. They could be financed partially by the UI system, in which case workers essentially draw part of the benefits they would have received if they had become unemployed.

Work-sharing policies have been currently adopted by 21 U.S. states. Yet, these have a limited public commitment to replace earnings, so the take-up is relatively low. Even though a large amount of layoffs have already taken place, if expanded, such programs could increase aggregate employment by reducing continuing layoffs at those firms that keep shedding workers.[11] Work sharing was also available to firms in Germany during the current recession, and has been credited to have helped avert a significant number of layoffs, despite a drop in GDP growth that was larger than the decline in the United States.[12] Clearly, it is important to pay attention to the details of such an arrangement. From the point of view of UI, being unemployed is a clearly defined state. For administering work sharing, it may be difficult to screen eligible firms. Yet, the successful implementation by many states suggests that these difficulties can be surmounted on a practical level.

The evaluation of work sharing is still at an early stage. However, it comes with lower financial involvement and less direct steering of economic activities than more targeted interventions, and is likely to extend the benefits of government support to a much broader group of workers. A related strategy to help avert layoffs of productive workers would be to create programs geared to maintain access to short-term credit to firms in financial distress that are otherwise economically viable. This approach would be most sensible in times of a sudden reduction in private credit, such as what occurred after the financial crisis in 2008.

A second approach would be to encourage workers and firms to find private solutions to reduce the risk of layoffs, such as work-time accounts based on an agreement between workers and firms to smooth hours over the business cycle. Thus, effectively the firm saves part of the overtime pay on behalf of workers during good economic times, and draws down balances when economic conditions worsen instead of firing the worker. In addition to work sharing, such work-time accounts were a major factor in keeping layoffs to a minimum in Germany during the current recession. The use of these accounts was particularly prevalent in sectors that exhibited stable growth prior to the crisis and were experiencing shortages in skilled labor (Möller 2010). Such an arrangement is based on long-term relationships between workers and firms that involve some degree of firm- or sector-specific skills. While the paradigm in the United States is one of high labor turnover, many employment relationships are long-lasting, and employers invest in searching for and training workers. Thus, in light of the large costs of job displacement, such arrangements may be beneficial to both workers and firms.[13]

Clearly, layoffs cannot be prevented altogether and are to some extent a natural feature of a market economy. However, in special circumstances, such as the financial crisis of 2008 or high interest rates in 1982, some layoffs might occur at otherwise healthy firms, leading to costly layoffs as productive employment relationships are severed. Similarly, layoffs in declining industries might be accelerated, leading to large-scale layoffs that exceed the capacity of the labor market to reallocate these workers. For such cases, mechanisms that allow firms to avoid large-scale layoffs could prevent large and lasting consequences affecting a high number of workers. The potential benefit of such safeguards is underscored by the difficulty of alleviating the long-term consequences of workers affected by layoffs and unemployment.

## CONCLUSION

An increasing number of studies indicate that job loss and unemployment during recessions can impose large and lasting costs on affected workers and their families. The short-term burden of these costs can be alleviated relatively cost-effectively, such as by extending UI. Less is known about how to help workers adjust to the significant long-term costs. While cost-effective policies exist to reintegrate the long-term unemployed into the labor market, the potential for policy interventions to reduce long-term earnings losses appears less promising. Given the large long-term costs of layoffs and unemployment, preventive measures to avoid large-scale layoffs in future recessions are worth exploring further.

### Notes

This chapter is based on a testimony before the Joint Economic Committee of U.S. Congress on April 29, 2010, on "Long-Term Unemployment: Causes, Consequences and Solutions," as well as a presentation at the Reconnecting to Work conference at the University of California–Los Angeles.

1. Davis and von Wachter (2012) contrast the effects of job loss in booms and recessions. Farber (2005) provides estimates of the short-term costs of job loss for the United States over the past two decades. Couch and Placzek (2010), Kodrzycki (2007), Schoeni and Dardia (2003), and von Wachter, Handwerker, and Hildreth (2008) show medium-run estimates for California, Connecticut, and Massachusetts in the early 1990s.
2. Estimates of the cost of job loss are robust to extensive controls for worker and

firm characteristics; the effect of layoffs is not larger when firms displace fewer workers, such as during smaller layoffs or good economic times.

3. For a more technical overview, see Meyer (2002).

4. This point is made by Chetty (2008), who estimates that over half of employment effects of UI may be due to such an income effect.

5. The take-up rate of UI fluctuates between 40 and 50 percent for all unemployed and between 70 and 80 percent among job losers (Congressional Budget Office 2004). A similar back of the envelope calculation and caveat is made by Elsby, Hobijn, and Şahin (2010, Section 3.2).

6. Landais, Michaillat, and Saez (2010) discuss the role of aggregate factors in determining the employment effects of UI extensions; Rothstein (2011) provides estimates suggesting small to moderate employment effects of UI extensions in the United States during the Great Recession of 2008.

7. For example, for an assessment of the effect of wage subsidies, see Perloff and Wachter (1979) and Congressional Budget Office (2010). For an assessment of the effect of training programs for displaced workers see U.S. Department of Labor (1995, Section 5). For a meta-analysis of the effect of various labor market policies, see Card, Kluve, and Weber (2010).

8. While the average returns from training are positive, relatively few displaced workers take up training (Jacobson, Lalonde, and Sullivan 2005).

9. U.S. Department of Labor (1995, Section 5). For a survey of recent evidence see Jacobson (2009).

10. This has been recently advocated under the name of *wage insurance*, for example, by Kling (2006); Jacobson, Lalonde, and Sullivan (1993); and Litan and Kletzer (2001). Evidence on related *reemployment bonus experiments* suggests that short-term subsidies raise employment, but may only be cost-effective if targeted to workers most likely to exhaust their benefits (O'Leary, Decker, and Wandner 2005; U.S. Department of Labor 1995).

11. This argument is spelled out in Hassett's (2010) testimony to the House Committee on Financial Services.

12. Burda and Hunt (2011) and Möller (2010) assess the role of work sharing and work-time accounts in averting layoffs in Germany.

13. A small theoretical literature discusses why such contracts are not prevalent in the United States (Grossman and Hart 1983; Ramey and Watson 1997).

# References

Autor, David H., and Mark G. Duggan. 2006. "The Growth in the Social Security Disability Rolls: A Fiscal Crisis Unfolding." *Journal of Economic Perspectives* 20(3): 71–96.

Baker, George, Michael Gibbs, and Bengt Holmstrom. 1994. "The Wage Policy of a Firm." *Quarterly Journal of Economics* 109(4): 881–919.

Beaudry, Paul, and John DiNardo. 1991. "The Effect of Implicit Contracts on the Movements of Wages over the Business Cycle." *Journal of Political Economy* 99(4): 665–688.

Blanchard, Olivier Jean, and Lawrence F. Katz. 1992. "Regional Evolutions." *Brookings Papers on Economic Activity* 1(1992): 1–75.

Browning, Martin, and T. F. Crossley. 2001. "Unemployment Insurance Levels and Consumption Changes." *Journal of Public Economics* 80(1): 1–23.

Burda, Michael, and Jennifer Hunt. 2011. "What Explains the German Labor Market Miracle in the Great Recession?" *Brookings Papers on Economic Activity* 102(Spring): 273–335.

Burgard, Sarah A., Jennie E. Brand, and James S. House. 2007. "Toward a Better Estimation of the Effect of Job Loss on Health." *Journal of Health and Social Behavior* 48(4): 369–384.

Card, David, Jochen Kluve, and Andrea Weber. 2010. "Active Labor Market Policy Evaluations: A Meta-Analysis." *Economic Journal* 120(548): F452–F477.

Chan, Sewin, and Ann Huff Stevens. 2001. "Job Loss and Employment Patterns of Older Workers." *Journal of Labor Economics* 19(2): 484–521.

Charles, Kerwin Kofi, and Melvin Stephens. 2004. "Disability, Job Displacement and Divorce." *Journal of Labor Economics* 22(2): 489–522.

Chetty, Rajeev. 2008. "Moral Hazard Versus Liquidity and Optimal Unemployment Insurance." *Journal of Political Economy* 116(2): 173–234.

Congressional Budget Office (CBO). 2004. *Family Income of Unemployment Insurance Recipients.* Washington, DC: CBO.

———. 2007. *Long-Term Unemployment.* Washington, DC: CBO.

———. 2008. *Options for Responding to Short-Term Economic Weaknesses.* Washington, DC: CBO.

———. 2010. *Policies for Increasing Economic Growth and Employment in 2010 and 2011.* Washington, DC: CBO.

Couch, Kenneth A., and Dana W. Placzek. 2010. "Earnings Losses of Displaced Workers Revisited." *American Economic Review* 100(1): 572–589.

Davis, Steven J., and Till von Wachter. 2012. "Recessions and the Cost of Job Loss." *Brookings Papers on Economic Activity* 103(Fall): 1–72.

Elsby, Michael, Bart Hobijn, and Aysegul Şahin. 2010. "The Labor Market in the Great Recession." *Brookings Papers on Economic Activity* 100(Fall): 1–69.

Farber, Henry S. 2005. "What Do We Know about Job Loss in the United States? Evidence from the Displaced Workers Survey, 1984–2004." *Economic Perspectives* (Spring): 13–28.

Grossman, Sanford, and Oliver Hart. 1983. "Implicit Contracts under Asymmetric Information." *Quarterly Journal of Economics* 98(Supplement): 123–156.

Gruber, Jonathan. 1997. "The Consumption Smoothing Benefits of Unemployment Insurance." *American Economic Review* 87(1): 192–205.

Hassett, Kevin A. 2010. "Prospects for Employment Growth: Is Additional Stimulus Needed?" Testimony before the House Committee on Financial Services. February 23, Washington, DC: American Enterprise Institute for Public Policy Research.

Jacobson, Louis S. 2009. "Strengthening One-Stop Career Centers: Helping More Unemployed Workers Find Jobs and Build Skills." The Hamilton Project Discussion Paper No. 2009-01. Washington, DC: Brookings Institution.

Jacobson, Louis, Robert LaLonde, and Daniel G. Sullivan. 1993. "Earnings Losses of Displaced Workers." *American Economic Review* 83(4): 685–709.

———. 2005. "Estimating the Returns to Community College Schooling for Displaced Workers." *Journal of Econometrics* 125(1–2): 271–304.

Kahn, Lisa. 2010. "The Long-Term Labor Market Consequences of Graduating from College in a Bad Economy." *Labour Economics* 17(2): 303–316.

Kling, Jeffrey. 2006. "Fundamental Restructuring of Unemployment Insurance: Wage-Loss Insurance and Temporary Earnings Replacement Accounts." The Hamilton Project Discussion Paper No. 2006-05. Washington, DC: Brookings Institution.

Kodrzycki, Yolanda K. 2007. "Using Unexpected Recalls to Examine the Long-Term Earnings Effects of Job Displacement." Federal Reserve Bank Working Paper No. W07-2. Boston, MA: Federal Reserve Bank of Boston.

Kondo, Ayako. 2008. "Differential Effects of Graduating during Recessions across Race and Gender." Photocopy. New York: Columbia University.

Landais, Camille, Pascal Michaillat, and Emmanuel Saez. 2010. "Optimal Unemployment Insurance over the Business Cycle." NBER Working Paper No. 16526. Cambridge, MI: National Bureau of Economic Research.

Litan, Robert, and Lori Kletzer. 2001. "A Prescription to Relieve Worker Anxiety." Brookings Institution Policy Brief No. 73. Washington, DC: Brookings Institution.

Machin, Steven, and Alan Manning. 1999. "The Causes and Consequences of Long-Term Unemployment in Europe." In *Handbook of Labor Economics Vol. III*, Orley Ashenfelter and David Card, eds. Amsterdam: Elsevier, pp. 3085–3139.

Meyer, Bruce. 2002. "Unemployment and Workers' Compensation Programmes: Rationale, Design, Labour Supply and Income Support." *Fiscal Studies* 23(1): 1–49.

Möller, Joachim. 2010. *The German Labor Market Response in the World Recession—Demystifying a Miracle.* Nuremburg, Germany: Institut für Arbeitsmarkt- und Berufsforschung.

Neal, Derek. 1995. "Industry-Specific Human Capital: Evidence from Displaced Workers." *Journal of Labor Economics* 13(4): 653–777.

———. 1999. "The Complexity of Job Mobility among Young Men." *Journal of Labor Economics* 17(2): 237–261.

O'Leary, Christopher J., Paul T. Decker, and Stephen A. Wandner. 2005. "Cost-Effectiveness of Targeted Reemployment Bonuses." *Journal of Human Resources* 40(1): 270–279.

Oreopoulos, Philip, Marianne Page, and Ann Huff Stevens. 2008. "The Intergenerational Effects of Worker Displacement." *Journal of Labor Economics* 26(3): 455–483.

Oreopoulos, Philip, Till von Wachter, and Andrew Heisz. 2012. "The Short- and Long-Term Career Effects of Graduating in a Recession." *American Economic Journal: Applied Economics* 4(1): 1–29.

Oyer, Paul. 2008. "The Making of an Investment Banker: Macroeconomic Shocks, Career Choice, and Lifetime Income." *The Journal of Finance* 63(6): 2601–2628.

Parent, Daniel. 2000. "Industry-Specific Capital and the Wage Profile: Evidence from the National Longitudinal Survey of Youth and the Panel Study of Income Dynamics." *Journal of Labor Economics* 18(2): 306–323.

Perloff, Jeffrey M., and Michael L. Wachter. 1979. "The New Jobs Tax Credit: An Evaluation of the 1977–1978 Wage Subsidy Program." *American Economic Review* 69(2): 173–179.

Poletaev, Maxim, and Chris Robinson. 2008. "Human Capital Specificity: Evidence from the Dictionary of Occupational Titles and Displaced Worker Surveys, 1984–2000." *Journal of Labor Economics* 26(3): 387–420.

Ramey, Garey, and Joel Watson. 1997. "Contractual Fragility, Job Destruction, and Business Cycles." *Quarterly Journal of Economics* 112(3): 873–911.

Rege, Mari, Kjetil Telle, and Mark Votruba. 2009. "The Effect of Plant Downsizing on Disability Pension Utilization." *Journal of the European Economic Association* 7(4): 754–785.

Rothstein, Jesse. 2011. "Unemployment Insurance and Job Search in the Great Recession." Brookings Papers on Economic Activity. Washington, DC: Brookings Institution.

Rupp, Kalman, and David Stapleton. 1995. "Determinants of the Growth in the Social Security Administration's Disability Programs: An Overview." *Social Security Bulletin* 58(4): 43–70.

Schmieder, Johannes, and Till von Wachter. 2010. "Does Wage Persistence

Matter for Employment Fluctuations? Evidence from Displaced Workers." *American Economic Journal: Applied Economics* 2(3): 1–21.

Schmieder, Johannes, Till von Wachter, and Stefan Bender. 2012a. "The Effects of Extended Unemployment Insurance over the Business Cycle: Regression Discontinuity Estimates over 20 Years." *Quarterly Journal of Economics* 127(2): 701–752.

———. 2012b. "The Effect of Unemployment Insurance Extensions on Re-employment Wages." Photocopy. New York: Columbia University.

Schoeni, Robert, and Michael Dardia. 2003. *Estimates of Earnings Losses of Displaced Workers Using California Administrative Data.* PSC Research Report No. 03-543. Ann Arbor, MI: Population Studies Center, University of Michigan.

Stevens, Ann Huff. 1997. "Persistent Effects of Job Displacement: The Importance of Multiple Job Losses." *Journal of Labor Economics* 15(1, Part 1): 165–188.

Stevens, Ann Huff, and Jesamyn Schaller. 2009. "Short-Run Effects of Parental Job Loss on Children's Academic Achievement." NBER Working Paper No. 15480. Cambridge, MA: National Bureau of Economic Research.

Sullivan, Daniel, and Till von Wachter. 2009. "Job Displacement and Mortality: An Analysis Using Administrative Data." *Quarterly Journal of Economics* 124(3): 1265–1306.

Topel, Robert, and Michael Ward. 1992. "Job Mobility and the Careers of Young Men." *Quarterly Journal of Economics* 107(2): 439–479.

U.S. Department of Labor, Office of the Chief Economist. 1995. *What's Working (and What's Not): A Summary of Research on the Economic Impacts of Employment and Training Programs.* Washington, DC: U.S. Department of Labor.

von Wachter, Till, Jae Song, and Joyce Manchester. 2011a. "Long-Term Earnings Losses Due to Mass-Layoffs during the 1982 Recession: An Analysis Using Longitudinal Administrative Data from 1974 to 2004." Photocopy. New York: Columbia University.

———. 2011b. "Trends in Employment and Earnings of Allowed and Rejected Social Security Disability Insurance Program Applicants." *American Economic Review* 101(7): 3308–3329.

von Wachter, Till, and Elizabeth Weber Handwerker. 2009. "Variation in the Cost of Job Loss by Worker Skill: Evidence Using Matched Data from California, 1991–2000." Photocopy. New York: Columbia University.

von Wachter, Till, Elizabeth Weber Handwerker, and Andrew Hildreth. 2008. "Estimating the 'True' Cost of Job Loss: Evidence Using Matched Data from California 1991–2000." Center for Economic Studies Working Paper No. 09-14. Washington, DC: U.S. Census Bureau.

# 3
# Labor Market Policy in the Great Recession

## Lessons from Denmark and Germany

John Schmitt
*Center for Economic and Policy Research*

The Great Recession started in the United States, but it quickly spread to the rest of the world. Although some countries fared even worse than the United States, many have weathered the crisis better. This chapter reviews the experience of 21 rich countries that are all members of the Organisation for Economic Co-operation and Development (OECD)—a group of economies that offer a standard of living roughly comparable to that of the United States—in search of possible lessons for the United States.

Figure 3.1 shows the percentage point change between 2007 and 2009 in the unemployment rate across these 21 rich countries. Since national definitions of the unemployment rate vary somewhat, the figure uses "harmonized" unemployment rates prepared by the OECD. It covers a period that starts in 2007—the year just before the downturn hit most economies—and ends in 2009—the year that the economy reached its trough in most countries.[1] The United States had the third-highest increase in unemployment (4.7 percentage points), after Spain (9.7 percentage points) and Ireland (7.2 percentage points). In the other OECD economies, the increase in unemployment was less than 2.5 percentage points. Strikingly, the unemployment rate actually fell in Germany (−1.2 percentage points).

Economic theory suggests three possible reasons for the different unemployment experience. The first is that the size of the negative demand shock might have varied across these economies. It could be, for example, that Spain suffered a larger negative demand shock than the United States, which in turn experienced a worse demand shock than

**Figure 3.1 Change in Harmonized Unemployment Rate, 2007–2009**

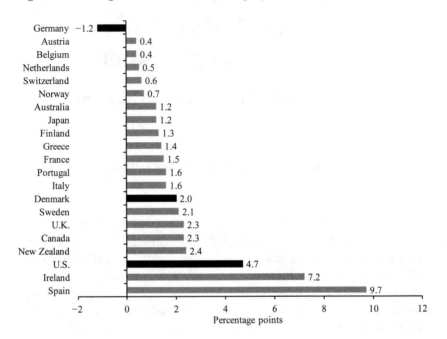

SOURCE: OECD.

most of the rest of the OECD. Since we can't directly observe demand shocks, we can never be completely sure. But all of the evidence—primarily the change in GDP—suggests that the demand shocks were large and negative across all of these economies. The shock to Germany, for example, was likely larger than the one that hit the United States: between 2007 and 2009, German GDP fell 3.8 percent, compared to a 2.6 percent decline in the United States.[2]

A second possible explanation for the different unemployment experiences is different macroeconomic policy responses. Even if all countries experienced exactly the same negative demand shock, countercyclical macroeconomic policy—expansionary monetary and fiscal policy—could have reduced the observed decline in GDP more in some countries than in others. Macroeconomic policy responses did vary widely across the OECD, but most analyses suggest that the United States did better than average.[3] The Federal Reserve Board lowered interest rates farther and faster in the United States than, for example, the European Central Bank did in Europe.[4] The United States also implemented the largest explicit fiscal stimulus package (as a share of GDP) among the major OECD countries. Other countries passed smaller stimulus packages, and automatic stabilizers were more important parts of the fiscal response elsewhere, but, even taking all these measures into account, the fiscal response was likely faster and larger in the United States.

A final possible explanation for the different international unemployment experience in the downturn is the structure of labor markets. National labor market institutions likely vary in the way that they translate a given decline in GDP into unemployment. The preceding discussion suggests that the United States experienced a negative demand shock somewhere in the middle of the OECD experience and responded in a way that partly mitigated the negative impact of that shock. If so, the large rise in U.S. unemployment suggests that U.S. labor market institutions offered a particularly harsh trade-off between falling GDP and unemployment. By contrast, Germany appears to have experienced a larger negative demand shock and responded to that shock with less aggressive monetary and fiscal policy than the United States, yet unemployment *declined* in Germany between 2007 and 2009. The German labor market institutions appear to have handled the demand shock extremely well.

This chapter will focus on this third possible reason for international differences in the labor market response to the Great Recession: national labor market institutions. The following section presents a brief framework for thinking about how labor market institutions and policies mediate the relationship between GDP and employment. The next section reviews the experience of two national economies: Denmark, which operated what was arguably the most successful labor market of the 2000s, and Germany, which has had remarkable success in resisting the international rise in unemployment since 2007. The final section concludes with some possible lessons for the United States.

## LABOR MARKETS AND MACROECONOMIC SHOCKS

Once a negative demand shock has hit and macroeconomic policy has been deployed in response, the path of employment and unemployment depends largely on the labor market. For the 21 rich OECD countries, Figure 3.2 graphs the change between 2007 and 2009 in the unemployment rate against the corresponding change in real GDP. Over this two-year period, real GDP fell in every country except Austria.

Figure 3.2 includes a regression line that traces the average relationship between unemployment and GDP across the countries. Most of the countries in the sample (including Denmark) are clustered close to the average experience. These data suggest that the national labor market institutions in place in these countries converted a 1 percentage point decline in GDP into about a 0.4 percentage point increase in unemployment. Several of the countries, however, lie well off the line, indicating that they differ substantially from the OECD average. Germany, for example, falls well below the regression line. Any given decline in German GDP had far less impact on the unemployment rate than at the OECD average. The United States, Spain, and Ireland, meanwhile, all lie well above the regression line, suggesting that GDP declines in these countries are much more costly in terms of unemployment than was the case for the OECD in general.

In broad terms, labor markets can adjust to macroeconomic demand shocks in some combination of two ways (with an important caveat, which will follow). Either employment can fall—fewer workers working the same number of hours as before (at the same hourly wage) meet the new lower output demanded—or average hours per worker can fall—the same number of workers spend fewer hours per week to produce the new output level.[5]

Imagine that a particular decline in aggregate demand requires that employers reduce their total wage bill by 10 percent. The wage bill ($B$) is equal to the total number of employees ($E$), times the average number of hours they work ($H/E$), times the average hourly wage ($W$):

$$B = E \times (H/E) \times W .$$

**Figure 3.2 Unemployment and GDP, 2007–2009**

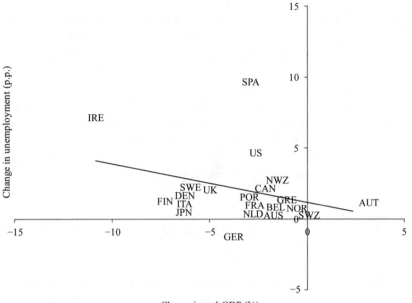

Change in real GDP (%)

SOURCE: Author analysis of OECD and Conference Board data.

Employers could cut the wage bill by reducing employment by 10 percent (*E*), or by reducing the average hours per worker (*H/E*) by 10 percent (or, of course, by some combination of the two). As the discussion below suggests, labor market institutions play a crucial role in determining exactly where the adjustment falls. In Denmark, the United States, and most other countries in the OECD, much of the adjustment has fallen on employment (*E*), resulting in substantial increases in unemployment. In Germany, essentially all of adjustment has occurred through changes in average hours (*H/E*), resulting in a counterintuitive decline in unemployment there.

One caveat applies, however. These adjustment mechanisms are incomplete on their own. One of the central insights of Keynes's *General Theory* (1936) was that cuts in workers' incomes, whatever form they take, cannot restore full employment in the face of a shortfall in aggregate demand. The very action of individual employers cutting workers' take-home pay in order to bring their individual wage bills into line with the lower level of aggregate demand has the effect of further lowering aggregate demand. Labor market adjustments take place, but in the middle of an aggregate demand slump, they cannot restore full employment without offsetting expansionary macroeconomic policy or some new, positive aggregate demand shock. This new, positive demand shock could take many forms, some of which are more desirable than others. The short U.S. recession of 2001, for example, ended primarily because of demand fueled by the housing bubble. Economists have long argued, however, that wage-led growth offers a more sustainable avenue for reviving and maintaining aggregate demand (see Berg and Ostry [2011], Coats [2011], Kalecki [1991], and Palley [2011]).

## THE GREAT RECESSION IN DENMARK AND GERMANY

Labor market institutions have been at the center of the discussion of labor market performance since at least the 1980s, when unemployment rose sharply and remained stubbornly high in most of the major OECD economies. A standard view, encapsulated in the OECD's 1994 *Jobs Study*, maintains that labor market institutions are the primary determinant of labor market performance. In this framework, labor market institutions should first and foremost seek to maximize "flexibility"; other economic and social goals of labor market institutions—including economic security and equity—are distinctly secondary. This view generally leaves aside the role that macroeconomic policy plays in the smooth functioning of the labor market. To the extent that this approach does acknowledge the importance of macroeconomics, it is usually to argue that institutions such as unions, UI, and employment protection legislation restrict the effectiveness of macroeconomic policy by introducing "rigidities" that channel expansionary policies toward inflation, not job creation.[6]

In the mid-2000s, this standard view was updated and amended in the face of substantial evidence that countries with what qualified as "rigid" labor markets by many of the usual indicators (high union coverage rates, generous unemployment benefits, and strong employment protection legislation) were performing quite well.[7] This new thinking brought explicit recognition to two key ideas. The first was that the previous understanding of flexibility was too narrow. Unemployment insurance, for example, might reduce incentives for the unemployed to accept jobs, but these same benefits might improve the quality of eventual job matches by giving workers more time to search. A second key idea was that the interaction of labor market institutions matters more than the specific institutions separately. In some contexts, high unemployment benefits might raise the unemployment rate. In others, the existence of generous unemployment benefits might persuade workers and unions to accept lower levels of legal employment protection, resulting in a more, not less, dynamic labor market.

The rest of this section reviews the recent experience of two countries with very different experiences before and after the Great Recession. Denmark had what was arguably the OECD's best performing labor markets before the Great Recession, but has suffered since 2008. German labor markets, meanwhile, were generally struggling shortly after unification until the end of 2007, when suddenly Germany began to outperform every major economy in the OECD.

## DENMARK

The experience of the Danish economy from the mid-1990s through the Great Recession did a great deal to change the consensus view on the need for labor market "flexibility" at all costs (see, for example, OECD [2004, 2006] and European Commission [2006]). In 2007, just before the downturn, the Danish unemployment rate was 4.0 percent (compared to 4.6 percent in the United States), and the employment-to-population rate was 77.1 percent (compared to 71.8 percent in the United States).[8] Low-wage work was rare, and income inequality was near the lowest levels in the OECD (see Mason and Salverda [2010]; OECD [2011, Figure 1]; and Westergaard-Nielsen [2008]). Yet, by OECD standards, Denmark had high taxes, high unionization rates, generous unemployment benefits, and a costly system of education, training, assistance, and incentives for unemployed workers.

The Danish model—often described as being built around *flexicurity*—worked, it seems, because it combined a high level of flexibility for employers with equally high levels of security for workers. The flexibility came primarily in the form of low levels of legal employment protections combined with a willingness of Danish unions to accept lay-offs. The security came in the form of high wages, strong unions, and generous UI and other benefits.[9] A defining Danish labor market institution has been its collection of active labor market policies (ALMPs). These policies, targeted at unemployed workers, include education and training, extensive assistance in job search, financial incentives, subsidized employment, and, in some cases, even direct public-sector employment. Active labor market policies increase flexibility by moving the unemployed through the generous unemployment benefits system and enhance security by improving skills and providing temporary, subsidized employment opportunities for workers who otherwise might spend long periods unemployed.

From about the middle of the 1990s through the onset of the Great Recession, the system produced enviable results. The unemployment rate fell rapidly, from over 10 percent in 1993 to less than 5 percent by 2000, a range where it remained until 2008. Most accounts explain these results by emphasizing the way that the flexicurity institutions supported a dynamic labor market that was capable of rapidly reallocating workers from firms and sectors in the economy where demand was falling to firms and sectors where demand was on the rise (see OECD [2004, 2006] and European Commission [2006]). Politically, the system worked because workers and their unions felt secure enough about their incomes to agree to only limited legal and negotiated job security. Employers accepted the higher taxes and an important economic role for unions because these were the political conditions that made the greater numerical flexibility possible.

Figures 3.3–3.7 put the salient features of the Danish system into international perspective. As Figure 3.3 shows, Denmark has an exceptionally large commitment to ALMPs. The share of national GDP spent on ALMPs (per percentage point of unemployment) was the highest in the OECD.[10] Using this standard measure, in 2007, before unemployment in Denmark increased, the country spent 0.26 percent of GDP per percentage point of unemployment—about 12 times more than the United States (0.02 percent of GDP per point of unemployment) and about 5 times more than Germany (0.05).

**Figure 3.3  Expenditure on Active Labor Market Policies, 2007**

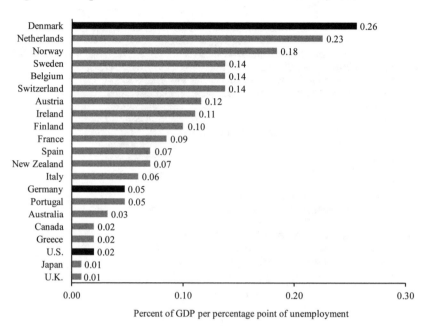

Percent of GDP per percentage point of unemployment

SOURCE: Author analysis of OECD data.

One of the standard justifications for the large scale of Danish ALMPs is that they are necessary to ensure that the unemployed don't get stuck in the country's generous, union-administered, unemployment benefit system. The OECD data in Figure 3.4 support the view that unemployment benefits in Denmark are fairly generous by international standards. An average worker receives about 70 percent of the average wage during their initial period of unemployment, slightly less generous than Germany (74 percent), but more generous than the United States (58 percent).[11]

Denmark is also heavily unionized. As Figure 3.5 shows, over 80 percent of Danish workers are covered by a collective bargaining agreement, more than in Germany (63 percent), and far above the level in the United States (13 percent).

At the same time, Denmark provides a relatively low level of legal employment protection. Figure 3.6 presents an index of the strength of

**Figure 3.4  Generosity of Unemployment Insurance**

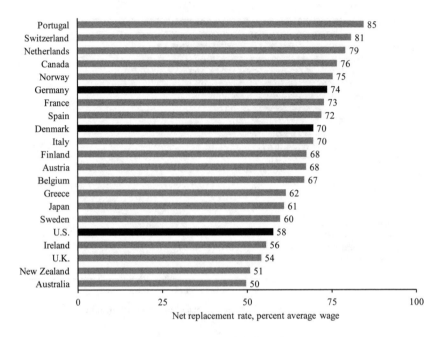

SOURCE: Author analysis of OECD data.

employment protection legislation (EPL) based on the OECD's assessment of legal and bargained conditions on severance pay, advance notification of dismissal, legal procedures related to unfair dismissal, and related issues. The index runs from zero (essentially no legal employment protections) to six (a very high level of legal employment protection). On this scale, Denmark (1.6) lies closer to the English-speaking economies (Ireland, New Zealand, Australia, Canada, the United Kingdom, and the United States) than it does to Germany (3.0), Sweden (2.9), and France (2.5), where employment protections are stronger.

This combination of institutions performed well between the middle of the 1990s and the onset of the Great Recession. These same institutions, however, have not fared so well in the current downturn. Figure 3.7 compares the increase between 2007 and 2010 in the unemployment rate in Denmark, Germany, the United States, and Spain (the OECD

**Figure 3.5  Collective Bargaining Coverage, 2007**

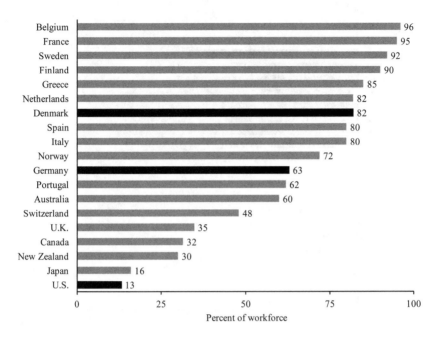

SOURCE: Visser, ITCWSS data, http://www.uva-aias.net/208.

country with the largest increase in unemployment over the period). Between 2007 and 2010, the Danish unemployment rate almost doubled from 4.0 to 7.8 percent, more closely tracking the experience of Spain and the United States than of Germany.

Figure 3.8 sketches the labor market adjustment path in Denmark between 2007 and 2009. Total employment and total hours worked increased about 2 percent between 2007 and 2008—the crisis hit Denmark later than most of the rest of the OECD. Between 2008 and 2009, however, total employment and total hours both fell sharply. Total hours fell to about 2 percent below their 2007 level, with almost all of this reduction in total hours stemming from a decline in the total number of workers. The Danish economy did not adjust to the labor-demand shock by lowering the average number of hours worked by the existing workforce, but rather primarily by reducing the number of workers, with

**Figure 3.6  Employment Protection Legislation, Regular Employment, 2008**

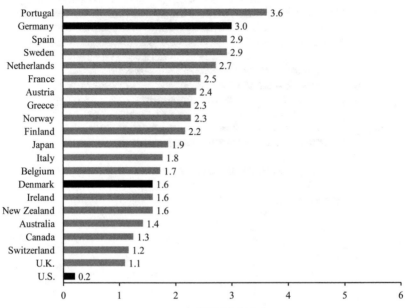

SOURCE: OECD.

relatively small cuts in the average hours worked. In the framework discussed earlier, almost all of the adjustment fell on employment cuts and very little on average hours reductions.

Why did the Danish system suddenly lose its luster? One explanation is that the same institutions that created a dynamic labor market in good macroeconomic times acted to accelerate job loss during the downturn. Low dismissal costs produced dynamism when there was sufficient macroeconomic demand to produce full employment. However, low dismissal costs encouraged employers to reduce employment (rather than hours) when aggregate demand fell. Meanwhile, the country's superb system of ALMPs was poorly equipped to deal with aggregate demand slumps. The majority of ALMPs seek to "activate" unemployed workers through training or by connecting them with available jobs. Even the best ALMPs, however, cannot connect workers to jobs if there are no jobs.

**Figure 3.7 Change in Unemployment Rate, 2007–2010**

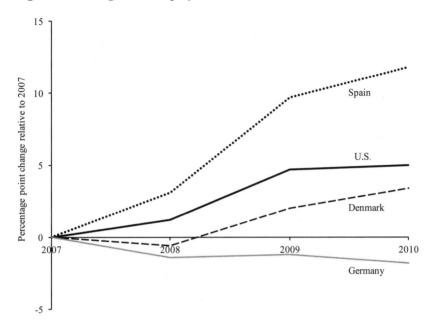

SOURCE: Author analysis of OECD data.

The Danish model worked well when aggregate demand was high enough to ensure full employment. When the economy was operating near full employment, the main economic bottlenecks were on the supply side of the labor market (labor quality, the distribution of skills, and location of workers relative to jobs). When the bottlenecks were on the demand side, however, greater numerical flexibility did little to generate employment and helped to drive unemployment up. A real danger for Denmark going forward is that the cyclical flaws in the model will be used to dismantle rather than reform these institutions. The German case suggests that a combination of numerical flexibility—in hours—combined with moderate legal and bargained dismissal costs can produce far better outcomes in downturns. This experience should inform efforts to improve the ability of Danish institutions to respond to future periods of slack demand.

**Figure 3.8  Change in Hours and Employment, Denmark, 2007–2009**

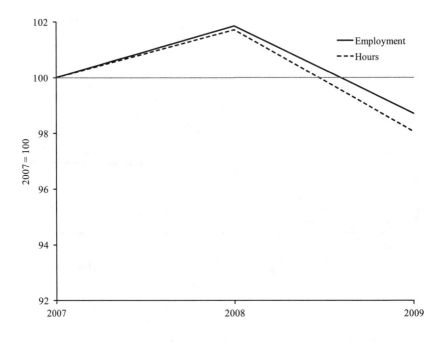

SOURCE: Author analysis of OECD data.

## GERMANY

Before the Great Recession, Germany was not the ideal model of labor market performance. Unemployment was high, job creation was weak, and wage inequality was on the rise, primarily because of the sharp rise in low-wage and precarious employment that began in the mid to late 1990s.[12] German companies were profitable and the country was a successful exporter, but the labor market was generally not delivering. The German labor market's performance since the Great Recession, however, has been remarkable. In 2007, before the downturn, the German unemployment rate was 8.7 percent (using the OECD's internationally comparable measure, which differs slightly from the official German rate); by 2009, when the rest of the world was feeling the worst of the economic crisis, the unemployment rate in Germany had fallen to 7.5 percent.

The German unemployment rate dropped because labor market adjustment fell entirely on hours, not employment (or wages). Figure 3.9 shows the change in hours and employment between 2007 and 2009. The contrast with Denmark is striking. The Great Recession affected both countries later than in the United States, but once the downturn hit, total hours fell in Germany—to about 98 percent of 2007 levels—even as total employment remained constant. Effectively, reductions in the average hours worked absorbed all of the decline in labor demand in Germany. By contrast, in Denmark the reduction in labor demand fell strongly on total employment, with only small reductions in average hours worked per employee.

How did Germany manage this? A key element was the German system of short-time work (STW) programs, which provide part-time

**Figure 3.9  Change in Hours and Employment, Germany, 2007–2009**

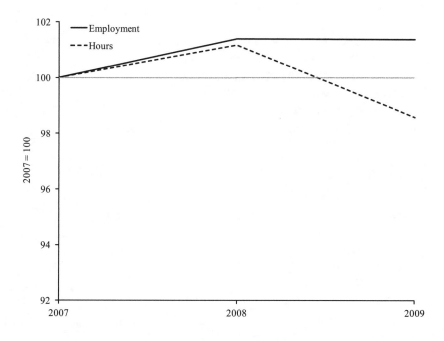

SOURCE: Author analysis of OECD data.

unemployment benefits to workers who have had their hours reduced in response to declines in demand for their employers' products and services.[13] In a traditional UI program, if an employer needs to cut employment by 20 percent in the wake of a demand shock, the employer will lay off 20 percent of workers who, assuming that they individually meet eligibility requirements, will receive UI benefits. In a STW system, the same employer could instead cut average hours for all employees by 20 percent, and each employee (again, assuming individual eligibility requirements are met) would receive 20 percent of the full-time UI benefit. Germany had a long-standing STW system in place before the downturn, and participation increased rapidly by the end of 2008 (International Labor Organization [ILO] 2011, Figure 3.5). By 2009, Germany had one of the highest shares of its workforce enrolled in STW programs (see Figure 3.10).

Short-time work, however, was only part of the hours adjustment in Germany. According to an analysis by Fuchs et al. (2010) of the change

**Figure 3.10  Short-Time Work, 2009**

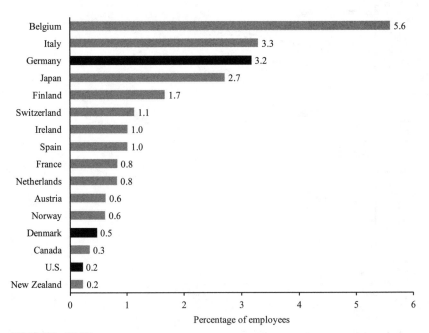

SOURCE: OECD.

in the average hours worked between 2008 and 2009, STW accounted for about 25 percent of the decline in average hours (see Table 3.1).[14] Employer-initiated reductions in working time—usually implemented through collective-bargaining agreements—were even more important than STW, accounting for about 40 percent of the decrease in hours. Another 20 percent of the decline in hours was due to the debiting of workers' working-time accounts. About two-thirds of German companies have working-time accounts in place, where employees who work more than the normally scheduled number of hours (or work weekends, evenings, and holidays, or under other circumstances) can "bank" these hours against future hours of work.[15] In the recession, many employers—with the agreement of workers and their unions—cut hours worked and paid workers out of the hours accumulated in these working-time accounts, rather than laying them off. Reductions in overtime accounted for an additional 20 percent of the decline in average hours worked.

A review of the German experience suggests that several institutional features pushed employers to reduce hours rather than workers. Relatively high levels of legal employment protection (see Figure 3.6) made it more expensive for firms to lay workers off than to reduce hours. Relatively high levels of collective-bargaining coverage (see Figure 3.5), combined with a union focus on job security, further raised the relative cost of layoffs. The widespread presence of collective bargaining facilitated hours flexibility by implementing negotiated working-time banks and allowing for negotiated reductions in overtime and the usual workweek. Together, this institutional structure gave substantial incentives to firms to prefer hours reductions to employment cuts, and gave workers incentives to do the same.

Germany faces its own set of institutional challenges. Critics of the German response to the Great Recession have argued that the strong

**Table 3.1 Average Hours Reductions in Germany, 2008–2009 (%)**

| Proportion of average hours reduction due to: | |
|---|---|
| Increased short-time work | 25 |
| Employer-initiated reductions in working time | 40 |
| Debiting working-time accounts | 20 |
| Reduced overtime | 20 |

NOTE: Factors are approximate and therefore do not sum to 100.
SOURCE: OECD (2010) analysis of Fuchs et al. (2010).

emphasis on "labor hoarding" at the firm level may mean that the economy is not efficiently reallocating labor from firms and sectors that are lagging to those that are growing. This argument, however, assumes that the problem facing German firms in the downturn is their individual or industry performance, rather than an across-the-board collapse in demand. In some respects, though, this concern presents the mirror image of the problem facing Denmark. The German system, as implemented since 2008, has done an excellent job coping with a deep recession, but a reliance on hours adjustments alone could conceivably create efficiency problems when the economy is operating closer to full employment. If an individual firm is facing a long-term decline in demand for its output, for example, it is not likely to be socially efficient —beyond a transition period—to adjust to that firm-specific decline in demand by keeping workers tied to the declining firm. But, this kind of reasoning suggests modifying the functioning of the STW system in good times, so as to ensure that STW does not impede the efficient reallocation of workers across firms and sectors when the economy is operating near full capacity. In fact, the German STW system already appears to incorporate this kind of flexibility across the business cycle. Before the downturn, participation in STW was limited to six months, but as the economy deteriorated, the maximum duration of STW was expanded successively to 12, 18, and then 24 months (ILO 2011).

## LESSONS FOR THE UNITED STATES

The recent experiences of Denmark and Germany provide important insight into the interplay between labor market institutions and business cycles. Danish institutions—built around numerically flexible employment levels and strong income security for workers—appear to perform well when the economy is at or near full employment. In good times, the country's expensive ALMPs work to connect unemployed workers to available jobs. In a severe downturn in which the overwhelming cause of unemployment is a lack of aggregate demand, however, institutions that encourage adjustment through employment are a liability, and policies that seek to "activate" workers are not particularly effective. Meanwhile, German institutions, which act to keep workers connected to their current employers, may have drawbacks when the economy is operating near full employment because they may discourage the efficient reallocation of workers from firms and industries where demand is falling to firms and industries where demand is on the rise. These same institutions, however, appear to have been well-suited for coping with the Great Recession because they encouraged firms to cut hours rather than workers, sharing the burden of the downturn more widely and helping firms keep their workforces in place and ready for the subsequent upturn.

In the United States, the hours and employment response to the Great Recession looked more like it did in Denmark than Germany. The recession hit U.S. labor markets slowly at first, but between 2008 and 2009, employment and hours both fell sharply (see Figure 3.11). By 2009, employment was about 4 percent lower than it had been in 2007, and total hours were down almost 6 percent. The larger drop in hours

**Figure 3.11  Change in Hours and Employment, United States, 2007–2009**

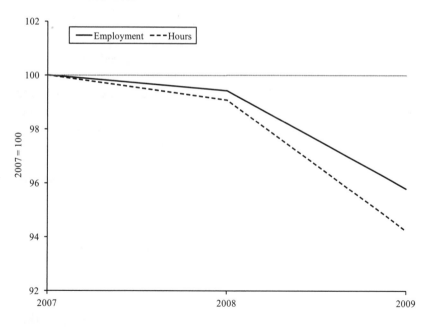

SOURCE: Author analysis of OECD data.

than in employment implies that some of the labor market adjustment in the United States fell on the average number of hours worked. Employment losses, however, still accounted for the large majority of the adjustment. A simple decomposition suggests that the mix of declines in employment and in average hours worked was similar in the United States and Denmark. In both countries, about 30 percent of the decline in total hours was the result of a decline in average hours per employee, and about 70 percent was the result of lower levels of employment.[16]

The hours decline in the United States largely reflected a rise in part-time work for economic reasons, reductions in overtime, and reductions in the average hours of full-time employees. Overall, U.S. labor market institutions did little to encourage firms to reduce average hours rather than employment levels. On the one hand, firing costs are low: the United States has the lowest level of employment protection (see Figure 3.6) and the lowest level of collective bargaining coverage (see Figure 3.5) in the OECD. On the other hand, the structure of employer-provided benefits, particularly health insurance, make hours cuts a less cost-effective tool for lowering total compensation. While 17 states operated short-time unemployment compensation programs during the Great Recession, take-up rates were too low to have a measureable impact on national average hours worked. At their peak, participation rates in STW programs, for example, never exceed a few tenths of a percent of the total U.S. workforce (see Figure 3.10).[17]

Are there any direct lessons that the United States can learn from the experience of Denmark and Germany? The political debate around "structural unemployment"—the idea that unemployment has remained high because workers lack the skills in demand in the postrecession economy—has rekindled an interest in education and training as a means to rescue the labor market in the short term.[18] Yet, on a per-unemployed-worker basis, Denmark spends more than 12 times what the United States does to train and "activate" unemployed workers, with only moderately better outcomes since the beginning of the downturn. In general, supply-side ALMP strategies seem poorly suited to recessions caused by deficient demand. At least with respect to performance in an aggregate demand slump, the Danish system appears to emulate a lot of the least desirable features of the U.S. system, including low firing costs that encourage firms to adjust to downturns by cutting workers rather than hours.

The German response to the downturn, in contrast, suggests that labor market institutions that encourage hours reductions rather than layoffs can spread the pain of adjustment more equitably, as well as act to preserve good matches between workers and firms. German institutions raise the cost of firing workers—through employment protection legislation and collective bargaining agreements—and encourage reductions in average hours—through STW arrangements, withdrawals from collectively bargained working-time accounts, and collectively bargained reductions in the usual workweek and overtime.

Translating these lessons to the U.S. context, however, is a challenge. Firing costs are low in the United States, and the two main avenues for raising firing costs—employment protection legislation or a rapid expansion in collective bargaining—appear unlikely in the foreseeable future. Individual states could expand the use of STW programs within their UI systems, but the scale of expansion necessary would be substantial and would require addressing a host of concrete barriers that keep take-up rates low (Vroman and Brusentsev 2009).

A federal program to subsidize temporary reductions in work hours—by giving tax credits to employers who implement or expand paid sick days, paid family leave, paid vacations, four-day workweeks, or other practices that reduce hours—instead of, or in addition to, expanding state-level UI programs might also help.[19] One advantage of a temporary federal tax break for these practices is that such a system directly targets the high cost of cutting hours relative to cutting workers, which has limited the take-up rate for STW programs in the United States. Even in Germany, which has higher firing costs and a long-standing STW system, STW accounted for only about one-fourth of the decline in average hours.

In labor markets, at least, the Great Recession continues. Given the political discussion around debt and deficits, any further macroeconomic policy response to the ongoing problems in the labor market seems unlikely. That leaves the United States little choice but to learn what it can from the labor market experiences of other countries that are also facing the worst downturn since the Great Depression. Unfortunately, U.S. labor market institutions have fared much worse than the OECD average since 2007, turning any given decline in GDP into far more unemployment than almost every major economy in the OECD. To the extent that U.S. policymakers have decided on any course of action, it appears to be, in President Obama's words, to "win the future" by investing in education and training. The experience of Denmark, which won the future in the 1990s and 2000s, however, gives cause for caution. Education, training, and other measures to connect workers to jobs only work when there are jobs to be had. For the immediate future, the experience of Germany looks to offer a better way forward. German labor market institutions gave employers incentives to spread the pain across the full workforce, with the remarkable result that the unemployment rate there actually fell over the course of the Great Recession.

## Notes

The author thanks Eileen Appelbaum, Lauren Appelbaum, Dean Baker, Nicole Woo, and participants at the Institute for Research on Labor and Employment conference on Reconnecting to Work at the University of California–Los Angeles, especially Wayne Vroman and Jeffrey Wenger, for many helpful comments. Thanks also to Sairah Husain for research assistance, and the Ford Foundation and the Open Society Institute for financial support for this research.

1. The National Bureau of Economic Research marks the beginning of the recession in the United States at December 2007, with the trough in June 2009. The downturn generally hit the rest of the world later, in 2008. For a summary of the timing of the recession in European economies, see Cameron (2010, Table 2).
2. The German economy was particularly vulnerable to the Great Recession because world trade collapsed in the downturn and exports are such an important part of the German economy. The main source of the shock in the United States was the collapse in the residential housing market. Construction and real-estate-related employment plummeted, but the main blow came through the (still not quite complete) deflation of the housing bubble, which greatly reduced household net worth and induced a severe contraction in spending. See, for example, Baker (2009a) and Bivens (2011).
3. See, for example, OECD (2009) and ILO (2009). For a dissenting view on comparative fiscal policy, see Aizenman and Pasricha (2011), but note that their definition of fiscal stimulus is narrow, excluding tax cuts and increases in unemployment benefits, for example.
4. For an illustration of key interest rates across a sample of the major OECD economies, see ILO (2011, Figure 2.2).
5. A third possibility is that total employment and average hours remain constant, but the hourly wage falls. Assuming that average productivity remains constant, however, the wage cut alone doesn't lower output to match the new lower level of demand facing the firm.
6. For a summary of the debate and a critique of the orthodox view, see, among

many others, Howell (2005), Schmitt and Wadsworth (2005), and Baccaro and Rei (2007).

7. For a succinct summary of the amended thinking, see OECD (2006, Chapter 3).

8. Rate is for population ages 15–64; see OECD (2010, Table B).

9. The Danish UI system is administered by the country's unions, not the government.

10. Expenditures (as a share of GDP) per percentage point of unemployment is a standard measure of the generosity of national ALMP programs. Using only expenditures (as a share of GDP) would exaggerate the generosity of ALMP programs in the case of countries with high levels of unemployment. In the case of Denmark, dividing the total expenditures (as a share of GDP) by the unemployment rate emphasizes that the Danish system is exceptionally generous—per unemployed worker.

11. The figure shows the OECD's estimate of the (unweighted) average net replacement rate during the "initial phase of unemployment" for a worker at average earnings across six family types. These results are conditional on receipt of benefits, that is, the generosity estimate does not factor in the share of the unemployed who are eligible for and take up unemployment benefits. In the current downturn, take-up rates in the United States have been as high as three-fourths; in normal times, including earlier recessions, the take-up rate in the United States is typically between one-third and one-half.

12. For a discussion of German and related European economic policy and performance since reunification, see Bosch and Weinkopf (2008), Carlin and Soskice (2009), Leschke and Watt (2010), Möller (2010), and Schettkat and Sun (2009).

13. For discussions of STW in Germany and elsewhere in the OECD, see Cahuc and Carcillo (2011), Hijzen and Venn (2011), ILO (2011), and Vroman and Brusentsev (2009).

14. The original analysis is in Fuchs et al. (2010). I rely here on the ILO's (2011) presentation of its findings.

15. For a helpful discussion in English of the German system, see Fagan, Hegewisch, and Pillinger (2006).

16. Between 2007 and 2009, total hours fell 5.8 percent and total employment fell 4.2 percent. The 4.2 percent decline in employment represents about 72 percent of the 5.8 percent decline in total hours, with about 28 percent accounted for by a decline in the average hours worked by the remaining workers. In Denmark, total hours fell 1.9 percent and total employment fell 1.3 percent, implying that employment declines accounted for about 68 percent and average-hours declines about 32 percent of the decline in total hours.

17. See Hijzen and Venn (2011, Figure 4). For a discussion of the limitations of existing U.S. short-time compensation programs, see Vroman and Brusentsev (2009) and Hijzen and Venn (2011).

18. For evidence against a large, permanent rise in the "natural" unemployment rate, see Daly, Hobijn, and Valletta (2011); Mishel (2011); Mishel, Shierholz, and Edwards (2010); Schmitt and Warner (2011); and Weidner and Williams (2011).

19. Baker (2009b,c) offers a proposal along these lines.

# References

Aizenman, Joshua, and Gurnain Kaur Pasricha. 2011. "Net Fiscal Stimulus during the Great Recession." NBER Working Paper No. 16779. Cambridge, MA: National Bureau of Economic Research. http://www.nber.org/papers/w16779 (accessed August 9, 2011).

Baccaro, Lucio, and Diego Rei. 2007. "Institutional Determinants of Unemployment: Does the Deregulatory View Hold Water?" *International Organization* 61(2): 527–569.

Baker, Dean. 2009a. *Plunder and Blunder: The Rise and Fall of the Bubble Economy*. Sausalito, CA: PoliPoint Press.

———. 2009b. *Pay for Play? Tax Credits for Paid Time Off*. Washington, DC: Center for Economic and Policy Research. http://www.cepr.net/documents/publications/pto-tax-credit-2009-03.pdf (accessed August 9, 2011).

———. 2009c. *Job Sharing: Tax Credits to Prevent Layoffs and Stimulate Employment*. Washington, DC: Center for Economic and Policy Research. http://www.cepr.net/documents/publications/job-sharing-tax-credit-2009-10.pdf (accessed August 9, 2011).

Berg, Andrew G., and Jonathan D. Ostry. 2011. "Inequality and Unsustainable Growth: Two Sides of the Same Coin?" IMF Staff Discussion Note SDN/11/08. Washington, DC: International Monetary Fund.

Bivens, Josh. 2011. *Failure by Design: The Story behind America's Broken Economy*. Ithaca, NY: Cornell University Press.

Bosch, Gerhard, and Claudia Weinkopf. 2008. *Low-Wage Work in Germany*. New York: Russell Sage Foundation.

Cahuc, Pierre, and Stephane Carcillo. 2011. "Is Short-Time Work a Good Method to Keep Unemployment Down?" IZA Discussion Paper No. 5430. Bonn: Institute for the Study of Labor.

Cameron, David R. 2010. "Fiscal Responses to the Economic Contraction." Unpublished paper. New Haven, CT: Yale University.

Carlin, Wendy, and David Soskice. 2009. "German Economic Performance: Disentangling the Role of Supply-Side Reforms, Macroeconomic Policy and Coordinated Economy Institutions." *Socio-Economic Review* 7(1): 67–99.

Coats, David, ed. 2011. *Exiting from the Crisis: Towards a Model of More Equitable and Sustainable Growth*. Brussels: European Trade Union Institute.

Daly, Mary, Bart Hobijn, and Rob Valletta. 2011. *The Recent Evolution of the Natural Rate of Unemployment*. San Francisco: Federal Reserve Bank of San Francisco. http://www.frbsf.org/publications/economics/papers/2011/wp11-05bk.pdf (accessed August 8, 2011).

European Commission. 2006. *Employment in Europe 2006*. Luxembourg: European Commission.

Fagan, Colette, Ariane Hegewisch, and Jane Pillinger. 2006. *Out of Time: Why Britain Needs a New Approach to Working-Time Flexibility*. London: Trade Union Congress.

Fuchs, J., M. Hummel, S. Klinger, E. Spitznagel, S. Wanger, and G. Zika. 2010. "Prognose 2010/2011: Der Arbeitsmarkt schließt an den vorherigen Aufschwung an." IAB-Kurzbericht no. 18. Nuremberg: IAB. I rely here on the ILO's (2011) presentation of their findings.

Hijzen, Alexander, and Danielle Venn. 2011. "The Role of Short-Time Work Schemes during the 2008–09 Recession." OECD Social, Employment and Migration Working Paper No. 115. Paris: OECD. http://dx.doi.org/10.1787/5kgkd0bbwvxp-en (accessed August 9, 2011).

Howell, David, ed. 2005. *Fighting Unemployment: The Limits of Free Market Orthodoxy*. Oxford: Oxford University Press.

International Labor Organization. 2009. *The Financial and Economic Crisis: A Decent Work Response*. Geneva: International Labor Organization.

———. 2011. *Germany: A Job-Centred Approach*. Geneva: International Labor Organization.

Kalecki, Michal. 1991. *Collected Works of Michal Kalecki, Capitalism: Economic Dynamics*. Vol. 2. Oxford: Clarendon Press.

Keynes, John Maynard. 1936. *The General Theory of Employment, Interest and Money*. New York: Harcourt, Brace.

Leschke, Janine, and Andrew Watt. 2010. "How Do Institutions Affect the Labour Market Adjustment to the Economic Crisis in Different EU Countries?" ETUI Working Paper 2010.04. Brussels: European Trade Union Institute.

Mason, Geoff, and Wiemer Salverda. 2010. "Low Pay, Working Conditions, and Living Standards." In *Low-Wage Work in the Wealthy World*, Jerome Gautie and John Schmitt, eds. New York: Russell Sage Foundation, pp. 35–90.

Mishel, Lawrence. 2011. *Reasons for Skepticism about Structural Unemployment: Examining the Demand-Side Evidence*. Washington, DC: Economic Policy Institute. http://epi.3cdn.net/c1218e8213c58051e4_tlm6b5tf9.pdf (accessed August 9, 2011).

Mishel, Lawrence, Heidi Shierholz, and Kathryn Edwards. 2010. *Reasons for Skepticism about Structural Unemployment*. Washington, DC: Economic Policy Institute.

Möller, Joachim. 2010. "The German Labor Market Response in the World Recession: De-mystifying a Miracle." *Zeitschrift für ArbeitsmarktForschung* 42(4): 325–336.

Organisation for Economic Co-operation and Development (OECD). 1994. *The OECD Jobs Study: Facts, Analysis, Strategies*. Paris: OECD.

———. 2004. *Employment Outlook*. Paris: OECD.

———. 2006. *Employment Outlook*. Paris: OECD.

———. 2009. *OECD Economic Outlook: Interim Report*. http://www.oecd.org/dataoecd/3/62/42421337.pdf (accessed August 9, 2011).

———. 2010. *Employment Outlook*. Paris: OECD.

———. 2011. *Growing Income Inequality in OECD Countries: What Drives It and How Can Policy Tackle It?* Paris: OECD. http://www.oecd.org/dataoecd/32/20/47723414.pdf (accessed August 9, 2011).

Palley, Thomas I. 2011. "A New Approach to Growth." In *Exiting from the Crisis: Towards a Model of More Equitable and Sustainable Growth*, David Coats, ed. Brussels: European Trade Union Institute, pp. 55–60.

Schettkat, Ronald, and R. Sun. 2009. "Monetary Policy and European Unemployment." *Oxford Review of Economic Policy* 25(1): 94–108.

Schmitt, John, and Jonathan Wadsworth. 2005. "Is the OECD Jobs Strategy behind U.S. and British Employment and Unemployment Success in the 1990s?" In *Fighting Unemployment: The Limits of Free Market Orthodoxy*, David Howell, ed. Oxford: Oxford University Press, pp. 156–196.

Schmitt, John, and Kris Warner. 2011. *Deconstructing Structural Unemployment*. Washington, DC: Center for Economic and Policy Research. http://www.cepr.net/documents/publications/dws-2011-03.pdf (accessed August 9, 2011).

Vroman, Wayne, and Vera Brusentsev. 2009. "Short-Time Compensation as a Policy to Stabilize Employment." Unpublished manuscript. Washington, DC: Urban Institute.

Weidner, Justin, and John C. Williams. 2011. *What Is the New Normal Unemployment Rate?* Federal Reserve Bank of San Francisco Economic Letter, February 14. San Francisco: Federal Reserve Bank of San Francisco. http://www.frbsf.org/publications/economics/letter/2011/el2011-05.html (accessed August 9, 2011).

Westergaard-Nielsen, Niels. 2008. *Low-Wage Work in Denmark*. New York: Russell Sage Foundation.

# 4
# Causality in the Relationship between Mental Health and Unemployment

Timothy M. Diette
*Washington and Lee University*

Arthur H. Goldsmith
*Washington and Lee University*

Darrick Hamilton
*The New School*

William Darity Jr.
*Duke University*

Unemployment is costly to society and individuals. Fifty years ago economist Arthur Okun (1962) demonstrated that for the United States in the postwar period, a 1 percent increase in the unemployment rate is associated with a 3 percent decline in gross national product. Subsequent work (Moosa 1997) revealed that this rule of thumb, known as Okun's Law, closely characterizes most developed economies. At the individual level, unemployed persons who are laid off experience financial losses in the form of a drop in income, even if they are covered by UI. Moreover, when reemployed, their wages typically fall short of their previous level for a number of reasons, one of which is that workers' skills are not fully portable across firms, occupations, and industries (Goldsmith and Veum 2002).

Social scientists also assert that unemployment lasting more than a few weeks is damaging to mental health. For instance, two meta-analytic studies (McKee-Ryan et al. 2005; Paul and Moser 2009) report that unemployed persons have substantially poorer psychological well-being after controlling for a wide range of factors expected to influence emotional health. However, a largely unresolved issue is whether the poor mental health status associated with the unemployed is *caused* by their involuntary joblessness. The purpose of this chapter is to move toward resolution of that question. First, we offer a new method for identifying whether there is a causal link between exposure to unemployment and emotional well-being. Second, by using this identification strategy, and by drawing upon data from two large nationally representative data sources—the National Comorbidity Survey Replication (NCS-R) and the National Latino and Asian American Study (NLAAS)—we estimate the impact of both short-term and long-term unemployment on a broad measure of emotional health.

## UNEMPLOYMENT, PSYCHOLOGICAL HEALTH, AND CAUSALITY

Social psychologists have proposed a number of pathways whereby involuntary joblessness potentially diminishes emotional well-being. Jahoda (1982) contends that unemployment is psychologically destructive primarily because it deprives an individual of the latent by-products of work, including a structured day, shared experiences, status, and opportunities for creativity and mastery.[1] Erikson (1959), in his life-span development theory, asserts that healthy emotional well-being as an adult is contingent upon the realization of occupational success for those intent on being breadwinners; therefore, unemployment is harmful to mental health. Attribution theory (Heider 1958; Weiner 1974) suggests that individuals seek an explanation for developments in their lives. Those who blame themselves for undesirable happenings such as involuntary joblessness are likely to experience feelings of "helplessness" (Seligman 1975), which damages mood (i.e., depression, anxiety) and self-perception.[2] Thus, for these persons, unemployment is expected to foster psychological distress. A number of psychologists and epidemiologists have asserted that the deleterious effects of unemployment increase as unemployment duration advances (Jackson and Warr 1984). They support the idea that stress accumulates, so there is reason to believe that each additional week of joblessness is even more emotionally damaging than prior weeks (Eisenberg and Lazarsfeld 1938; Harrison 1976). This suggests that long-term unemployment is more harmful to psychological well-being than short-term unemployment.

There is an extensive empirical literature dating to the Great Depression that documents a negative association between unemployment and psychological health.[3] Ethnographic studies conducted by Jahoda, Lazarsfeld, and Zeisel (1933) and Eisenberg and Lazarsfeld (1938) found that the unemployed exhibited both poor emotional well-being and an inferior view of themselves. Subsequently psychologists have developed inventories of questions designed to measure various dimensions of psychological health, including depression (Beck et al. 1961); anxiety (Spielberger et al. 1983); mastery or self-efficacy (Pearlin et al. 1981; Rotter 1966); self-esteem (Rosenberg 1965); and general psychiatric status (Goldberg and Blackwell 1970). Using these measures, numerous researchers conducting quantitative studies using cross-sectional survey data report that unemployed groups have lower levels of psychological well-being than employed groups. Unemployed persons have been found to exhibit higher levels of depression (Fryer and Payne 1986) and anxiety (Kessler, Turner, and House 1989), as well as lower levels of self-esteem (Feather 1982; Goldsmith, Veum, and Darity 1997) and self-efficacy (Goldsmith, Veum, and Darity 1995) compared to the employed.[4] However, because unemployment can be the consequence of poor mental health, it is not appropriate to interpret these results as conclusive evidence that unemployment causes deterioration in emotional well-being.

A common strategy to address the issue of reverse causality is to use longitudinal or panel data and examine whether changes in mental health coincide with changes in workforce status. The fundamental idea is that if involuntary joblessness leads to psychological distress, then persons moving from an employed to an unemployed state will exhibit a decline in mental health, and those switching over time from an unemployed to a working state will experience an improvement in psychological well-being. Numerous researchers report evidence consistent with this perspective. Their findings, although compelling, are not definitive evidence in favor of the hypothesis that unemployment causes deterioration in mental health.[5] The problem is that it is still possible that an individual's emotional well-being changed, for some reason, prior to the alteration in workforce status. We attempt to shed

further light on the question of causality by examining whether psychologically resilient persons (i.e., individuals who have always exhibited
sound emotional well-being) exposed to unemployment in the past year
are more likely to experience their first spell of poor emotional well-
being than persons employed throughout the past year.


## DATA AND A STRATEGY FOR DETERMINING IF
## UNEMPLOYMENT CAUSES POOR MENTAL HEALTH


### Data and Methodology

The NCS-R and the NLAAS were designed to collect information on potential determinants of mental disorders in the United States
through face-to-face interviews with respondents conducted in the pri-
vacy of their homes. The NCS-R was carried out on a nationally representative group of 9,282 racially and ethnically diverse respondents
between February 2001 and April 2003. The NLAAS contains information on a nationally representative group of 4,649 Latino or Asian
respondents collected between May 2002 and November 2003. These
data sets, which we merge together, are ideal to use in our investigation
of whether a causal link exists between unemployment and emotional
health because of the way that the survey collects respondent information on emotional well-being.

The NCS-R and the NLAAS respondents provided retrospective
information on whether they were sad, empty, discouraged, depressed,
or disinterested most of the day nearly every day for at least two weeks
or every month in the past year, which we use to construct a broad
measure of psychological distress.[6] An unusual and desirable feature of
the survey is that respondents who had suffered psychological distress
were asked to provide the year during which they first suffered a bout
of poor emotional health. We take advantage of this unique aspect of
the NCS-R and the NLAAS to develop a new strategy for assessing the
link between unemployment and psychological health. Using information on the year of first onset of poor psychological health, we stratify
our data into two separate subsamples or data sets. We construct a data
set composed of psychologically resilient persons (resilient)—those

who have either never experienced a significant bout of poor emotional well-being or had their first spell in the past year—and a second data set of psychologically vulnerable persons (vulnerable)—those who have experienced psychological distress in prior years.

The resilient subsample allows us to focus on those individuals without previous bouts of poor mental health. We suspect that persons who report never experiencing sustained psychological distress over the course of their life cycle and who are in the workforce will continue to be emotionally healthy. The resilient subsample allows us to analyze those least likely to have a bout of poor mental health leading to unemployment. Therefore, the findings of this subsample represent a significant step forward in resolving the problem of identifying a causal relationship between unemployment and poor mental health. However, there are conditions where the resilient subsample could still suffer from reverse causality.

For example, it is possible that some individuals in the resilient subsample are misclassified and should rightfully be in the vulnerable subsample. These individuals would need to represent a substantial portion of the resilient subsample to undermine the identification strategy. This would occur if there are many individuals who fail to report their prior poor mental health status because of poor recall, fail to recognize that they have mental health problems but their employers observe the problems, or the survey questions fail to identify those with mental health problems that employers observe. These individuals would be more likely to have a bout of poor mental health in the current year that causes unemployment. People may struggle to remember highly specific events, but the questionnaire is designed to identify general features of distress, such as being sad or feeling empty or discouraged. Therefore, we suspect that misclassification bias from failure to recall, poor recognition of their mental state, or inadequate questions is limited. A separate challenge to our identification strategy arises if a substantial group of individuals have mental health issues that are latent or dormant, these issues manifest themselves in the current year, or these individuals experience unemployment in the past 12 months as well. These individuals would be misclassified in our resilient subsample, belonging instead in the vulnerable subsample.

The data also contain information on the number of weeks during the past year that the respondent spent employed; unemployed; legitimately out of the labor force (i.e., disabled, retired, in school, or taking care of a family member); and discouraged or out of the labor force but not for justifiable reasons. We treat the latter category as time spent unemployed. Following the literature we classify those who spent 26 or more weeks unemployed during the past year as having suffered from long-term unemployment, while those who spent less time unemployed are designated as having experienced short-term unemployment.

Our primary interest is in examining the effect of involuntary unemployment on mental health. Therefore, persons who are out of the labor force for acceptable or genuine reasons are excluded from the data.[7] Thus, we focus our investigation on whether those who experience either short- or long-term unemployment in the past year had a higher probability of experiencing their first lifetime bout of emotional distress than those who spent the past year fully employed while holding constant other economic and social determinants of mental health.

## Descriptive Statistics

Our analysis is conducted separately on the subsample of resilient persons, those who have either never experienced a spell of prolonged psychological distress or have in the past year had their first bout of poor emotional health, and on the subsample of vulnerable individuals who have experienced sustained psychological distress prior to the past 12 months. Table 4.1 reveals that there are 5,485 persons in the resilient subsample, 5,421 of whom have never been "sad" or experienced a substantial period of poor mental health, while 64 individuals (slightly more than 1 percent of the subsample) were sad this past year for the first time. There are 2,109 respondents who have proven to be vulnerable to bouts of poor emotional well-being prior to the current year. Forty percent (845) of these persons also were saddled with psychological distress this past year, while 1,264 avoided poor mental health over the course of the previous 12 months.

Table 4.1 also presents information on labor force status for those who experienced psychological distress in the past year and for those who were emotionally healthy throughout the past 12 months, for both the resilient and vulnerable subsamples. Of interest is whether a disproportionate share of the individuals who are in distress this year experienced unemployment—especially long-term unemployment—over the past year.

**Table 4.1 History of Psychological Distress and Workforce Status Summary Statistics for Resilient and Vulnerable Subsamples**

| Panel A: Workforce status—resilient subsample ($n$ = 5,485) | | |
| --- | --- | --- |
| | Psychological distress this past year ($n$ = 64 = 1%) | No psychological distress this past year ($n$ = 5,421 = 99%) |
| Employed | 45 (70%) | 4,425 (82%) |
| Short-term unemployment | 5 (8%) | 383 (7%) |
| Long-term unemployment | 14 (22%) | 613 (11%) |

| Panel B: Workforce status—vulnerable subsample ($n$ = 2,109) | | |
| --- | --- | --- |
| | Psychological distress this past year ($n$ = 845 = 40%) | No psychological distress this past year ($n$ = 1,264 = 60%) |
| Employed | 619 (73%) | 1,051 (83%) |
| Short-term unemployment | 96 (12%) | 86 (7%) |
| Long-term unemployment | 130 (15%) | 127 (10%) |

NOTE: Resilient persons have either never experienced psychological distress—a sustained period over at least one month in the past year of sadness/discouragement/ disinterest—or had their first spell of distress in the past year. Vulnerable persons have experienced psychological distress prior to the past 12 months and may also have experienced a spell of distress in the past year. People who were unemployed in the past year and spent, in total, less than 26 weeks unemployed are identified as having experienced a bout of short-term unemployment. The long-term unemployed spent 26 or more weeks in the past year unemployed.

SOURCE: Data are drawn from the NCS-R and the NLAAS.

A large share (30 percent) of the persons in the resilient subsample who express being sad or distressed this year—for the first time in their lives—were exposed to unemployment during the past 12 months. Among those who experienced no psychological distress in the past year, only 18 percent spent some weeks unemployed. The same pattern exists for the vulnerable subsample. There is a higher proportion unemployed among those suffering poor emotional well-being in the past year (27 percent) relative to those with good emotional health in the most recent year (17 percent). Thus, it appears that involuntary job-lessness is associated with psychological distress, although caution is in order since we are not controlling for other determinants of emotional health that could be correlated with unemployment.

Psychologists expect a variety of social and economic factors to cushion the impact of unemployment on emotional health.[8] A valuable aspect of the NCS-R and the NLAAS data is the provision of information on a myriad of factors, both economic and social, that are believed to buffer the impact of unemployment on psychological health. This makes it possible to account for these features of a person's environment when examining the influence of unemployment on psychological health. The potential buffers that we are able to control for in our analysis include the number of siblings, the number of adult children, the extent of their wealth, and if the respondent has a parent who is still living, is currently married, has friends he speaks to often, and is part of a close-knit religious community. Table 4A.1 in Appendix 4A provides detailed definitions for all of the variables used in our formal analyses of psychological health.

The NCS-R and the NLAAS also provide extensive information on demographic factors that may contribute to psychological health, including a respondent's gender, educational attainment, age, and racial/ethnic heritage. Moreover, information is available on respondents' family characteristics when they were youths, allowing us to control for whether they were raised by both of their parents, whether the family received public assistance, and parents' education.

Appendix Table 4A.2 presents summary statistics on all of these variables used in our empirical analysis for both the resilient and vulnerable subsamples. We describe these characteristics below beginning with the resilient subsample. About half of the subsample is female (49 percent), 67 percent are married, 55 percent completed more than high school or are highly educated, 72 percent are more than 30 years old, 34 percent have young children in their homes, 44 percent are foreign born (unsurprising, since much of the data come from the NLAAS), and the average individual has accumulated $65,000 of net worth. The resilient subsample we analyze is very diverse with respect to race/ethnicity: 7 percent are African American, 34 percent are of Hispanic origin, 27 percent are Asian, and 32 percent are white. Most people were raised by both parents (79 percent), around half have highly educated mothers (49 percent) and fathers (47 percent), and only 4 percent grew up in poor families.

A third of the respondents in the resilient subsample had a mother who was still alive, and a quarter reported that their dad was still living. The typical person has 1.5 siblings and 1.3 adult children. Moreover, 45 percent say they speak to friends regularly and are frequent participants in a religious community. The characteristics of the vulnerable subsample are similar to those of the resilient subsample on a number of dimensions. However, the vulnerable group, relative to the resilient group, are only half as likely to be born outside the United States, more likely to be female (63 percent), more likely to have young children, less likely to be Asian, twice as likely to have grown up in a family on welfare, and have amassed substantially less wealth.

**Empirical Procedures**

In order to investigate the impact on emotional well-being of exposure to short- or long-term unemployment during the past year relative to employment throughout the past 12 months, we use Equation (4.1) to estimate the following model of psychological distress:

$$(4.1) \quad PsyDistress = \alpha + \beta(ShortTermUnem) + \psi(LongTermUnem) + \delta(\boldsymbol{Buffer}) + \lambda(\boldsymbol{X}) + \varepsilon.$$

*PsyDistress* takes on a value of 1 if the respondent reports being sad, empty, discouraged, depressed, or disinterested most of the day nearly every day for either at least two weeks or every month in the past year, otherwise it is 0. Two bivariate indicators are used to capture the extent of a person's unemployment experience over the past year. Those individuals who experienced some unemployment in the past year and the total number of weeks, whether or not they were concurrent, fall short of 26 weeks and are identified as having experienced short-term unemployment, in which case *ShortTermUnem* = 1. The variable *LongTermUnem* = 1 if an individual spent more than 25 weeks unemployed in the past year. *Buffer* is a vector containing social and economic support variables expected to mitigate or exacerbate the impact of involuntary joblessness on emotional health. $X$ is a vector of demographic and family control variables.

We estimate Equation (4.1) using a logistic regression to estimate the impact of unemployment and other factors on the odds that a person has suffered psychological distress in the past year. We report the odds ratios from the logistic regression. The odds ratios represent the effect of a unit increase in a continuous independent variable or a value of 1 for a bivariate variable on the odds of experiencing psychological distress in the past 12 months, relative to the odds when that same variable takes on a value of 0. A coefficient greater than 1 indicates an increase in the odds of suffering psychological distress (i.e., a coefficient estimate of 1.2 means a 20 percent increase in odds relative to when the bivariate variable is 0). A coefficient estimate of 1 suggests no change in the odds of poor emotional health occurring and a value less than 1 means the probability of poor emotional well-being in the past year is reduced (i.e., an estimate of 0.8 means the odds are 20 percent smaller relative to when the bivariate variable is zero).

For individuals in the resilient data set, the estimation of Equation (4.1) tests whether unemployment in the past year enhances the odds that a person will experience their first ever bout of sustained psychological distress in the past year. It is a commonly held belief that unemployment causes a decline in emotional well-being. The advantage of estimating Equation (4.1) with these data is that if unemployment is found to be associated with a greater likelihood of poor emotional health, the impact can be interpreted as causal with a high degree of confidence. Since these are resilient individuals who have only experienced their first bout of poor emotional health in the past year, it seems questionable that this bout of poor emotional health led to their current stretch of involuntary joblessness. A more likely story is that unemployment over the past year led to a deterioration of psychological well-being among persons with a history of sound psychological health.

In addition, to explore whether social and economic support mediates the impact of unemployment on contemporaneous emotional health, we stratify our subsamples by the presence (or not) of each buffer and reestimate the model.

# RESULTS

## Unemployment and Psychological Distress

Table 4.2 is a summary table that presents our estimates of the impact of both short- and long-term unemployment on the chances of experiencing psychological distress in the past year for the resilient subsample (Panel A) and the vulnerable subsample (Panel B). However, in our view reverse causality may mar the accuracy of the findings using the vulnerable population, while estimation of Equation (4.1) on a subsample of resilient persons may well purge the estimates of the endogeneity generated by reverse causality. Thus, the use of the resilient subsample can produce estimates that are capable of illuminating whether unemployment causes deterioration in emotional well-being. Model 1 is a sparse specification of Equation (4.1), where psychological distress is stipulated to depend solely on workforce status. Model 2 adds controls for a host of social and economic buffers. Model 3, the most complete specification, further augments the model to account for individual characteristics and family features when growing up. Full results for the resilient subsample are presented in Table 4A.3 in Appendix 4A, and Table 4A.4 reports our complete set of findings for the vulnerable subsample.

Panel A in Table 4.2 reveals that in all three models exposure to long-term unemployment in the past year significantly increases the odds that a resilient person will experience their first ever bout of poor emotional well-being in the current year relative to resilient individuals who were employed throughout the past year. The estimates range from a 125 percent increase in likelihood in Model 1 to a 218 percent increase in Model 2. However, those resilient persons who are subject to short-term unemployment during the past year have the same likelihood of experiencing their first bout of poor mental health as persons who were employed throughout the past year. Thus, our findings suggest that long-term unemployment has a larger detrimental impact on emotional health than bouts of short-term unemployment.

Recall that we classify people who have experienced poor mental health prior to the current year, regardless of the source of their poor emotional states, as vulnerable. Among these persons, exposure to

**Table 4.2 Logit Estimates of the Impact of Short-Term and Long-Term Unemployment on the Odds of Currently Experiencing Psychological Distress for Resilient and Vulnerable Subsamples—Summary Table**

| Variables | Model 1 Odds ratio | Model 2 Odds ratio | Model 3 Odds ratio |
|---|---|---|---|
| Panel A: Resilient subsample | | | |
| Workforce status | | | |
| Short-term unemployment | 1.28 | 1.10 | 1.04 |
| | (0.61) | (0.53) | (0.52) |
| Long-term unemployment | 2.25*** | 3.18*** | 2.85*** |
| | (0.69) | (0.99) | (0.96) |
| Observations | 5,485 | 5,485 | 5,485 |
| Panel B: Vulnerable subsample | | | |
| Workforce status | | | |
| Short-term unemployment | 1.90*** | 1.85*** | 1.80*** |
| | (0.30) | (0.29) | (0.29) |
| Long-term unemployment | 1.74*** | 1.69*** | 1.58*** |
| | (0.23) | (0.24) | (0.22) |
| Observations | 2,109 | 2,109 | 2,109 |
| Controls | | | |
| Buffers | No | Yes | Yes |
| Demographics & family factors | No | No | Yes |

NOTE: *** $p < 0.01$. Reference group for unemployment is employed throughout the previous year, those out of the labor force are excluded from the data, and discouraged workers are counted as unemployed. The set of buffer variables includes measures of assets, marital status, parents living, number of living siblings, number of adult children, having close friends, being part of a religious community, and the lack of young children in the home (see Table 4A.1 for detailed definitions of all variables included in the estimated models). Demographic controls include indicators for foreign born, gender, education level, age cohort, and racial and ethnic heritage. Family characteristics as a youth contain indicators that reveal who raised the respondent, their parents' education level, and the financial status of the family when the respondent was a youth. In addition, Models 2 and 3 include indicators for missing data on assets, number of siblings, talking on the phone with friends, and regular attendance at religious services.

SOURCE: Data are drawn from the NCS-R and the NLAAS.

either short- or long-term unemployment over the past year leads to a significant increase in their reporting to have experienced poor emotional health in the past year relative to similar persons who worked throughout the past year. For instance, vulnerable individuals who were subject to long-term unemployment were 58 percent more likely (Model 3) to experience psychological distress compared to those vulnerable persons in the labor force who worked the entire past year.

Consistent with our theory, we find that a number of buffers—being married, having adult children, having friends with whom you are in regular contact, and being part of a religious community—significantly reduce the odds of experiencing psychological distress over the past year, regardless of exposure to unemployment, for vulnerable persons (see Appendix Table 4A.4). However, emotional health does not appear to be directly related to such buffers for resilient persons.

## Do Buffers Mediate the Link between Unemployment and Psychological Distress?

An interesting question is whether social characteristics or features of a person's life act to insulate them from the adverse impact of unemployment on their psychological health. We explore this question by evaluating the link between unemployment and emotional well-being when a potential social buffer is present and when it is absent across both of our subsamples. Our findings for seven social buffers (i.e., being married or having a mother who is alive) are presented in Table 4.3. Table 4A.4 presents evidence on the prevalence of the various buffers in our data sets and on the size of the subsamples used to estimate the impact of unemployment on psychological health when a potential buffer is present and when it is absent.

Among resilient persons (the left side of Table 4.3), long-term unemployment is positively associated with the odds of experiencing psychological distress (i.e., an estimated coefficient > 1) in all seven cases when the buffer is not present (on 4 occasions the estimate is statistically significant), but also for 6 of the seven scenarios when the buffer is present (again, 4 of the estimated impacts are statistically significant). Moreover, the odds of poor emotional health due to long-term unemployment exposure are elevated to a greater extent when the buffer is not present relative to when it is present on three occasions

**Table 4.3  The Impact of Social and Economic Buffers on the Effect of Short-Term and Long-Term Unemployment on the Odds of Currently Experiencing Psychological Distress**

| | Resilient subsample | | Vulnerable subsample | |
|---|---|---|---|---|
| | Panel A: Marriage stratifications | | | |
| | Not married ($n = 1,732$) | Married ($n = 3,649$) | Not married ($n = 939$) | Married ($n = 1,170$) |
| Short-term unemployment | 1.63 (1.03) | 0.45 (0.48) | 2.61*** (0.63) | 1.30 (0.30) |
| Long-term unemployment | 4.03*** (2.00) | 1.92 (0.93) | 1.84*** (0.39) | 1.41* (0.28) |
| | Panel B: Mother stratifications | | | |
| | Mom not alive ($n = 3,531$) | Mom alive ($n = 1,731$) | Mom not alive ($n = 975$) | Mom alive ($n = 1,134$) |
| Short-term unemployment | 3.10* (1.92) | 0.49 (0.36) | 1.47 (0.41) | 1.99*** (0.40) |
| Long-term unemployment | 4.366*** (2.21) | 2.03 (1.01) | 1.45** (0.26) | 1.83** (0.44) |
| | Panel C: Father stratifications | | | |
| | Dad not alive ($n = 763$) | Dad alive ($n = 1,376$) | Dad not alive ($n = 607$) | Dad alive ($n = 851$) |
| Short-term unemployment | 1.75 (2.52) | 1.24 (0.72) | 1.79** (0.53) | 1.51* (0.37) |
| Long-term unemployment | 11.14*** (8.10) | 0.57 (0.60) | 1.98** (0.54) | 1.12 (0.34) |
| | Panel D: Adult children stratifications | | | |
| | No adult children ($n = 2,256$) | Adult children ($n = 2,845$) | No adult children ($n = 1,042$) | Adult children ($n = 1,067$) |
| Short-term unemployment | 0.84 (0.52) | 1.730 (1.38) | 1.59** (0.32) | 2.29*** (0.62) |
| Long-term unemployment | 2.34* (1.17) | 3.69** (1.92) | 1.19 (0.28) | 1.80*** (0.33) |

**Table 4.3 (continued)**

| | Resilient subsample | | Vulnerable subsample | |
|---|---|---|---|---|
| | Panel E: Talk to friends stratifications | | | |
| | Talk rarely ($n$ = 2,824) | Talk often ($n$ = 2,473) | Talk rarely ($n$ = 1,022) | Talk often ($n$ = 1,027) |
| Short-term unemployment | 1.12 (0.90) | 1.30 (0.81) | 1.56* (0.38) | 1.77** (0.39) |
| Long-term unemployment | 1.88 (1.06) | 4.26*** (1.87) | 1.72*** (0.35) | 1.40 (0.29) |
| | Panel F: Attend religious services stratifications | | | |
| | Attend rarely ($n$ = 2,472) | Attend regularly ($n$ = 2,292) | Attend rarely ($n$ = 1,011) | Attend regularly ($n$ = 864) |
| Short-term unemployment | 1.27 (0.75) | 0.71 (0.75) | 2.31*** (0.54) | 1.26 (0.38) |
| Long-term unemployment | 1.52 (0.88) | 4.44*** (2.34) | 1.91*** (0.38) | 1.30 (0.31) |
| | Panel G: Young children in the home stratifications | | | |
| | Children ($n$ = 1,054) | No children (426) | Children ($n$ = 626) | No children (1,483) |
| Short-term unemployment | 1.02 (0.81) | 0.99 (0.65) | 1.82* (0.56) | 1.79*** (0.36) |
| Long-term unemployment | 1.27 (1.05) | 3.53*** (1.43) | 1.03 (0.36) | 1.73*** (0.28) |

NOTE: *** $p < 0.01$, ** $p < 0.05$, * $p < 0.1$.
SOURCE: Data are drawn from the NCS-R and the NLAAS.

(marriage, mother alive, father alive), but for the other four social buffers the deleterious impact of long-term unemployment on emotional well-being is larger when the buffer is present. Thus, the evidence is mixed on whether social factors considered buffers reduce the impact of long-term unemployment on mental health for resilient persons. Furthermore, the results exhibit the same mixed pattern for the vulnerable population.

Short-term unemployment is essentially unrelated to psychological health regardless of whether social buffers are present or not for resilient individuals. Experiencing short-term unemployment only significantly damages emotional well-being for those without a mother who is alive in our resilient subsample. However, the situation is very different for the vulnerable who, prior to the current year, reported having suffered through bouts of poor emotional health. For them, whenever social buffers are not present, short-term unemployment leads to elevated odds of psychological distress, and in 6 out of 7 cases, the impact is statistically significant. The same pattern holds when the social barrier is present, which suggests that for vulnerable people the presence of what could well be a buffer does not mitigate the deleterious impact of short-term unemployment on mental health status. Thus, for persons with a prior history of poor emotional well-being, short-term unemployment exhibits the same negative pattern of effects on psychological health as long-term unemployment.

### Do Demographic Factors and Education Mediate the Link between Unemployment and Psychological Distress?

It is possible that the connection between psychological well-being and unemployment is influenced by demographic factors such as age and gender, as well as skill level or educational investment. To explore this possibility we stratified our data sets by gender, education level (more than high school, high school or less), and age (30 years of age or older, less than 30 years old). The results, reported in Table 4.4, offer three key insights. First, for the resilient individuals, short-term unemployment is unrelated to emotional well-being, regardless of gender, education level, or age cohort. Second, the results for the vulnerable individuals are consistent with the findings in Table 4.2, Panel B: both short- and long-term unemployment significantly damage mental health, regardless of gender, educational attainment, or age cohort. Finally, among the resilient population, those most negatively affected by long-term unemployment are males, highly educated, and older individuals—groups typically associated with being primary breadwinners.

### CONCLUSION

A longstanding belief among social scientists is that unemployment, especially long bouts, has deleterious effects on emotional health.

**Table 4.4  The Impact of Select Demographic Factors on the Effect of Short-Term and Long-Term Unemployment on the Odds of Currently Experiencing Psychological Distress**

| | Panel A: Gender stratifications | | | |
|---|---|---|---|---|
| | Resilient subsample | | Vulnerable subsample | |
| | Male ($n = 2,683$) | Female ($n = 2,349$) | Male ($n = 790$) | Female ($n = 1,319$) |
| Short-term unemployment | 0.59 (0.64) | 1.33 (0.82) | 1.94*** (0.49) | 1.78*** (0.38) |
| Long-term unemployment | 5.62*** (2.93) | 2.15* (0.98) | 1.93** (0.53) | 1.43** (0.24) |

| | Panel B: Education level stratifications | | | |
|---|---|---|---|---|
| | More than high school ($n = 2,933$) | High school or less ($n = 2,468$) | More than high school ($n = 1,234$) | High school or less ($n = 875$) |
| Short-term unemployment | 1.32 (0.93) | 0.75 (0.61) | 1.85*** (0.39) | 1.82** (0.47) |
| Long-term unemployment | 5.74*** (2.55) | 1.53 (0.73) | 1.42* (0.29) | 1.80*** (0.36) |

| | Panel C: Age stratifications | | | |
|---|---|---|---|---|
| | More than 29 ($n = 3,934$) | Less than 30 ($n = 1,443$) | More than 29 ($n = 1,565$) | Less than 30 ($n = 544$) |
| Short-term unemployment | 2.39 (1.33) | 0.26 (0.27) | 1.87*** (0.38) | 1.87** (0.52) |
| Long-term unemployment | 4.03*** (1.81) | 1.96 (1.09) | 1.63*** (0.26) | 1.21 (0.38) |

NOTE: *** $p < 0.01$, ** $p < 0.05$, * $p < 0.1$.
SOURCE: Data are drawn from the NCS-R and the NLAAS.

There is extensive evidence of a direct link between mental health and involuntary joblessness; however, the possibility that poor emotional well-being leads to long periods of unemployment has left the question of causality unresolved. This chapter introduces a new approach to the assembly of data that allows estimation of the link between emotional health and unemployment that may address concerns about the direction of causality. Our estimates are conducted using a subsample of resilient persons—those who until the current year have never experienced poor mental health. If resilient individuals are exposed to unemployment and exhibit poor mental health, it seems most likely that the joblessness harmed their psychological health. We find that long-term unemployment—but not short-term unemployment—promotes psychological distress among resilient persons. Moreover, the negative psychological consequences of long-term unemployment are present even when buffers exist, suggesting that policymakers consider both the monetary and nonpecuniary costs of unemployment when formulating policy to address economic downturns. Our findings suggest that the Great Recession and subsequent slow recovery have likely generated extraordinary negative psychological consequences: at the peak of this recession, about 45 percent of the unemployed had been out of work six months or longer, and one-third of the unemployed were jobless for at least a year.

## Notes

1. Warr's (1987) vitamin model is similar to Jahoda's (1982) functionality framework, in that desired features of work—like vitamins—contribute to psychological health, and when they are withheld or withdrawn through unemployment, emotional well-being is impaired.
2. Similarly, the Life Event model advanced by Brenner (1976) and Catalano and Dooley (1977) argues that any alterations in life circumstances, especially those deemed important to personal identity and status such as joblessness, are stressful and thus may hamper psychological health.
3. Poorer mental health status for the unemployed relative to the employed has been found for both men (Ensminger and Celentano 1990; Rowley and Feather 1987), and women (Dew, Bromet, and Penkower 1992), and long-term unemployment is especially damaging (Warr and Jackson 1985).
4. For a meta-analysis review of cross-sectional studies of the link between various forms of emotional health and unemployment, see Paul and Moser (2009).
5. For a meta-analytic review of longitudinal studies finding improvements in emotional health for unemployed who find work, see McKee-Ryan et al. (2005).
6. Kessler et al. (2003) combined respondents' self-reports on a similar set of feelings and emotions to construct a nonspecific psychological distress score to assess mental health.
7. Examples of acceptable reasons included those who are retired, homemakers, in school, and physically or mentally unable to work.
8. Numerous studies report that social support buffers the psychological distress associated with unemployment. See, for instance, Atkinson, Liem, and Liem (1986).

# Appendix 4A

**Table 4A.1  Definition of Variables Used in Logit Estimation of the
Influence of Unemployment on Psychological Distress**

| Variable name | Variable definition |
| --- | --- |
| Data sets | |
| Resilient | 1 if respondent has never experienced psychological distress (see outcome definition below) or had their first bout in the past year, 0 otherwise |
| Vulnerable | 1 if respondent has experienced psychological distress prior to the current year, 0 otherwise |
| Outcome | |
| PsyDistress | 1 if respondent reports being sad, empty, discouraged, depressed, or disinterested most of the day nearly every day in the past year for either at least two weeks or every month, 0 otherwise |
| Work force status | |
| Short-term unemployment | 1 if experienced unemployment during the past year and the total weeks summed to 25 or fewer weeks, 0 otherwise |
| Long-term unemployment | 1 if experienced unemployment during the past year and the total weeks summed to 26 or more weeks, 0 otherwise |
| Employed | 1 if employed throughout the past year at least 40 weeks and experienced no unemployment in past 12 months |
| Economic & social buffers | |
| Assets | Respondent's estimated value of assets less debts in thousands |
| Married | 1 if respondent is currently married or cohabitating, 0 otherwise |
| Mother living | 1 if respondent's biological mother is still alive, 0 otherwise |
| Father living | 1 if respondent's biological father is still alive, 0 otherwise |
| Siblings | Number of siblings respondent had while growing up, top coded at 8 |

**Table 4A.1  (continued)**

| Variable name | Variable definition |
|---|---|
| **Economic & social buffers** | |
| Adult children | Total number of adult children respondent has that are living—both biological and nonbiological, 0 otherwise. |
| Friends | 1 if respondent often talks on phone or gets together with friends most every day or a few times a week, 0 if less often. |
| Religious community | 1 if respondent attends religious services at least 3 times per month, 0 otherwise. |
| Young children | Total number of living biological and nonbiological children under 17 years of age living in respondent's home. |
| **Demographics** | |
| Foreign born | 1 if respondent reports being born outside the United States, 0 otherwise. |
| Female | 1 if respondent is female, 0 otherwise. |
| Highly educated | 1 if respondent reports having completed more than 12 years of formal education, 0 otherwise. |
| Young | 1 if respondent is less than 31 years of age, 0 otherwise. |
| African American | 1 if respondent reports being African Caribbean or African American, 0 otherwise. |
| Hispanic | 1 if respondent reports being Hispanic, 0 otherwise. |
| Asian | 1 if respondent reports being Asian, 0 otherwise. |
| **Family characteristics** | |
| Both parents | 1 if respondent reports being raised by both their biological father and biological mother, 0 otherwise. |
| Mother highly educated | 1 if respondent reports their mother completed 12 or more years of formal education, 0 otherwise. |
| Father highly educated | 1 if respondent reports their father completed 12 or more years of formal education, 0 otherwise. |
| Welfare | 1 if respondent reports their family was on welfare at some time during their youth, 0 otherwise. |

**Table 4A.2 Summary Statistics for All Variables Used in Logit Estimates for Resilient and Vulnerable Samples**

| Variable | Resilient ($n = 5,485$) | Vulnerable ($n = 2,109$) | Variable | Resilient ($n = 5,485$) | Vulnerable ($n = 2,109$) |
|---|---|---|---|---|---|
| PsyDistress | 0.01 (0.11) | 0.40 (0.49) | Young children | 0.34 (0.81) | 0.50 (0.95) |
| Short-term unemployment | 0.07 (0.26) | 0.09 (0.28) | Foreign born | 0.44 (0.50) | 0.21 (0.41) |
| Long-term unemployment | 0.11 (0.32) | 0.12 (0.33) | Female | 0.49 (0.50) | 0.63 (0.48) |
| Assets | 65.05 (163.43) | 75.25 (179.56) | Highly educated | 0.55 (0.50) | 0.59 (0.49) |
| Assets—missing | 0.38 (0.49) | 0.31 (0.46) | Young | 0.28 (0.45) | 0.26 (0.44) |
| Married | 0.67 (0.47) | 0.56 (0.50) | African American | 0.07 (0.25) | 0.07 (0.26) |
| Mother living | 0.35 (0.48) | 0.54 (0.50) | Hispanic | 0.34 (0.48) | 0.26 (0.44) |
| Father living | 0.26 (0.44) | 0.40 (0.49) | Asian | 0.27 (0.45) | 0.11 (0.31) |
| Father living—missing | 0.57 (0.51) | 0.31 (0.46) | Both parents | 0.79 (0.41) | 0.76 (0.43) |
| Siblings | 1.51 (2.29) | 2.37 (2.44) | Mother highly educated | 0.49 (0.50) | 0.59 (0.49) |
| Siblings—missing | 0.57 (0.50) | 0.30 (0.46) | Mother highly educated—missing | 0.11 (0.31) | 0.09 (0.29) |

| | | | | | |
|---|---|---|---|---|---|
| Adult children | 1.31 | 1.04 | Father highly educated | 0.47 | 0.52 |
| | (1.48) | (1.37) | | (0.50) | (0.50) |
| Friends | 0.45 | 0.49 | Father highly educated—missing | 0.20 | 0.19 |
| | (0.50) | (0.50) | | (0.40) | (0.39) |
| Friends—missing | 0.03 | 0.03 | Welfare | 0.04 | 0.08 |
| | (0.18) | (0.17) | | (0.20) | (0.28) |
| Religious community | 0.45 | 0.41 | Welfare-missing | 0.57 | 0.31 |
| | (0.50) | (0.49) | | (0.50) | (0.46) |
| Religious community—missing | 0.10 | 0.11 | | | |
| | (0.30) | (0.31) | | | |

SOURCE: Data drawn from the NCS-R and the NLAAS. Means are reported with standard errors in parentheses. Indicator variables are constructed that take on a value of 1 if the individual does not answer a question and therefore have a missing value and a value of zero for a valid response. We use the name construct of "variable name—missing" for each of these indicators. These indicators allow the observation to be included in the sample but not influence the coefficient of the related variable.

**Table 4A.3  The Impact of Short-Term and Long-Term Unemployment on the Odds of Currently Experiencing Psychological Distress for Resilient Individuals—Full Results**

| Variables | Model 1 Odds ratio | Model 2 Odds ratio | Model 3 Odds ratio |
|---|---|---|---|
| Workforce status | | | |
| Short-term unemployment | 1.28 | 1.10 | 1.04 |
| | (0.61) | (0.53) | (0.52) |
| Long-term unemployment | 2.25*** | 3.18*** | 2.85*** |
| | (0.70) | (0.99) | (0.96) |
| Buffers | | | |
| Assets | | 1.00 | 1.00 |
| | | (0.00) | (0.00) |
| Assets—missing | | 1.07 | 1.04 |
| | | (0.32) | (0.30) |
| Married | | 0.71 | 0.80 |
| | | (0.193) | (0.22) |
| Mother living | | 1.20 | 1.12 |
| | | (0.47) | (0.47) |
| Father living | | 1.30 | 1.12 |
| | | (0.46) | (0.42) |
| Father living—missing | | 0.10** | 0.03** |
| | | (0.10) | (0.04) |
| Siblings | | 1.03 | 1.02 |
| | | (0.07) | (0.07) |
| Siblings—missing | | 4.19 | 5.02 |
| | | (43.00) | (5.07) |
| Adult children | | 0.98 | 1.02 |
| | | (0.09) | (0.10) |
| Friends | | 1.01 | 0.99 |
| | | (0.26) | (0.26) |
| Friends—missing | | 0.50 | 0.46 |
| | | (0.38) | (0.36) |
| Religious community | | 0.69 | 0.64 |
| | | (0.19) | (0.18) |
| Religious community—missing | | 0.77 | 0.82 |
| | | (0.34 | (0.37) |
| Young children | | 1.15 | 1.16 |
| | | (0.11) | (0.13) |
| Born in foreign country | | 0.93 | 0.86 |
| | | (0.40) | (0.37) |

**Table 4A.3  (continued)**

| Demographics | | | |
|---|---|---|---|
| Female | | | 1.96** |
| | | | (0.55) |
| Highly educated | | | 0.87 |
| | | | (0.24) |
| Young | | | 1.42 |
| | | | (0.43) |
| African American | | | 1.45 |
| | | | (0.64) |
| Hispanic | | | 1.91* |
| | | | (0.76) |
| Asian | | | 1.64 |
| | | | (0.91) |
| Family characteristics | | | |
| Both parents | | | 1.08 |
| | | | (0.34) |
| Mother highly educated | | | 1.07 |
| | | | (0.39) |
| Mother highly educated—missing | | | 0.92 |
| | | | (0.46) |
| Father highly educated | | | 1.34 |
| | | | (0.47) |
| Father highly educated—missing | | | 0.95 |
| | | | (0.37) |
| Welfare | | | 0.69 |
| | | | (0.38) |
| Welfare—missing | | | 1.91 |
| | | | (2.00) |
| Constant | 0.01*** | 0.02*** | 0.01*** |
| | (0.01) | (0.01) | (0.01) |
| Observations | 5,485 | 5,485 | 5,485 |

NOTE: *** p < 0.01, ** p < 0.05, * p < 0.1. Resilient persons have either never experienced psychological distress—a sustained period over at least one month in the past year of sadness/discouragement/disinterest—or had their first spell of distress in the past year. Reference group for unemployment is employed throughout the previous year, those out of the labor force are excluded from the data, and discouraged workers are counted as unemployed. Indicator variables are constructed that take on a value of 1 if the individual does not answer a question and therefore have a missing value and a value of zero for a valid response. We use the name construct of "variable name—missing" for each of these indicators. These indicators allow the observation to be included in the sample but not influence the coefficient of the related variable.
SOURCE: Data are drawn from the NCS-R and the NLAAS.

**Table 4A.4  The Impact of Short-Term and Long-Term Unemployment
on the Odds of Currently Experiencing Psychological
Distress for Vulnerable Individuals—Full Results**

| Variables | Model 1 Odds ratio | Model 2 Odds ratio | Model 3 Odds ratio |
|---|---|---|---|
| Workforce status | | | |
| Short-term unemployment | 1.90*** | 1.85*** | 1.80*** |
| | (0.30) | (0.30) | (0.29) |
| Long-term unemployment | 1.74*** | 1.69*** | 1.58*** |
| | (0.23) | (0.24) | (0.22) |
| Buffers | | | |
| Assets | | 1.00*** | 1.00*** |
| | | (0.00) | (0.00) |
| Assets—missing | | 0.89 | 0.89 |
| | | (0.09) | (0.10) |
| Married | | 0.61*** | 0.63*** |
| | | (0.06) | (0.06) |
| Mother living | | 0.99 | 0.97 |
| | | (0.13) | (0.13) |
| Father living | | 0.97 | 0.99 |
| | | (0.12) | (0.13) |
| Father living—missing | | 1.86* | 1.71 |
| | | (0.61) | (0.59) |
| Siblings | | 1.01 | 0.99 |
| | | (0.03) | (0.03) |
| Siblings—missing | | 0.66 | 0.79 |
| | | (0.22) | (0.31) |
| Adult children | | 0.93** | 0.93** |
| | | (0.03) | (0.03) |
| Friends | | 0.77*** | 0.77*** |
| | | (0.07) | (0.07) |
| Friends—missing | | 0.73 | 0.69 |
| | | (0.21) | (0.20) |
| Religious community | | 0.82** | 0.84* |
| | | (0.08) | (0.08) |
| Religious community—missing | | 0.87 | 0.87 |
| | | (0.13) | (0.13) |
| Young children | | 1.03 | 1.01 |
| | | (0.05) | (0.05) |
| Born in foreign country | | 0.99 | 1.05 |
| | | (0.14) | (0.15) |

**Table 4A.4  (continued)**

| | | | |
|---|---|---|---|
| Demographics | | | |
| Female | | | 1.06 |
| | | | (0.10) |
| Highly educated | | | 0.88 |
| | | | (0.09) |
| Young | | | 1.21 |
| | | | (0.15) |
| African American | | | 1.11 |
| | | | (0.22) |
| Hispanic | | | 0.80 |
| | | | (0.15) |
| Asian | | | 0.71 |
| | | | (0.17) |
| Family characteristics | | | |
| Both parents | | | 0.92 |
| | | | (0.11) |
| Mother highly educated | | | 0.93 |
| | | | (0.11) |
| Mother highly educated—missing | | | 1.06 |
| | | | (0.20) |
| Father highly educated | | | 0.95 |
| | | | (0.12) |
| Father highly educated—missing | | | 1.06 |
| | | | (0.17) |
| Welfare | | | 1.46** |
| | | | (0.26) |
| Welfare—missing | | | 1.02 |
| | | | (0.33) |
| Constant | 0.59*** | 1.11 | 1.31 |
| | (0.03) | (0.22) | (0.35) |
| Observations | 2,109 | 2,109 | 2,109 |

NOTE: *** $p < 0.01$, ** $p < 0.05$, * $p < 0.1$. Vulnerable persons have experienced psychological distress—a sustained period over at least one month in the past year of sadness/discouragment/disinterest—or had their first spell of distress in the past year, prior to the past 12 months and may also have experienced a spell of distress in the past year. Reference group for unemployment is employed throughout the previous year, those out of the labor force are excluded from the data, and discouraged workers are counted as unemployed. Indicator variables are constructed that take on a value of 1 if the individual does not answer a question and therefore have a missing value and a value of zero for a valid response. We use the name construct of "variable name—missing" for each of these indicators. These indicators allow the observation to be included in the sample but not influence the coefficient of the related variable.

SOURCE: Data are drawn from the NCS-R and the NLAAS.

**Table 4A.5 Sample Size for Buffers and Demographics Used to Stratify the Data to Evaluate If the Impact of Unemployment on the Odds of Psychological Distress Depends on These Elements**

| Variable ($n$ prior to stratification) | Resilient subsample Variable status | | Variable ($n$ prior to stratification) | Vulnerable subsample Variable status | |
|---|---|---|---|---|---|
| | Yes | No | | Yes | No |
| Buffers | | | Buffers | | |
| Married ($n = 5,485$) | 66.5 | 33.5 | Married ($n = 2,109$) | 55.5 | 44.5 |
| Mother living ($n = 5,485$) | 34.6 | 65.4 | Mother living ($n = 2,109$) | 53.8 | 46.2 |
| Father living ($n = 2,356$) | 59.4 | 40.6 | Father living ($n = 1,458$) | 58.4 | 41.6 |
| Adult children ($n = 5,485$) | 58.9 | 41.1 | Adult children ($n = 2,109$) | 50.6 | 49.4 |
| Friends ($n = 5,297$) | 46.7 | 53.3 | Friends ($n = 2,049$) | 50.1 | 49.9 |
| Religious community ($n = 4,921$) | 49.8 | 50.2 | Religious community ($n = 1,875$) | 46.1 | 53.9 |
| Young children ($n = 5,485$) | 20.5 | 79.5 | Young children ($n = 2,109$) | 29.7 | 70.3 |
| Demographics | | | Demographics | | |
| Female ($n = 5,485$) | 48.9 | 51.1 | Female ($n = 2,109$) | 62.5 | 37.5 |
| Highly educated ($n = 5,485$) | 55.0 | 45.0 | Highly educated ($n = 2,109$) | 58.5 | 41.5 |
| Young ($n = 5,485$) | 28.3 | 71.7 | Young ($n = 2,109$) | 25.8 | 74.2 |

NOTE: Sample size prior to stratification may be smaller than the full subsamples used in the estimates presented in Tables 4.2 and 4.3. In the full subsamples, some observations contain missing values for specific buffers or demographics. Estimates with the full subsample include separate indicator variables for missing values for each variable. The stratification analysis eliminates observations with a missing value for the buffer or demographic variable that is the basis for stratifying the resilient or vulnerable subsamples.

# References

Atkinson, Thomas, Ramsay Liem, and Joan H. Liem. 1986. "The Social Costs of Unemployment: Implications for Social Support." *Journal of Health and Social Behavior* 27(4): 317–331.

Beck, Aaron T., Calvin H. Ward, M. Mendelson, J. Mock, and J. Erbaugh. 1961. "An Inventory for Measuring Depression." *Archives of General Psychiatry* 4(6): 561–571.

Brenner, M. Harvey. 1976. *Estimating the Social Costs of National Economic Policy: Implications for Mental and Physical Health and Clinical Aggression.* Report to the Joint Economic Committee of the U.S. Congress. Washington, DC: U.S. Government Printing Office.

Catalano, Ralph, and C. David Dooley. 1977. "Economic Predictors of Depressed Mood and Stressful Life Events." *Journal of Health and Social Behavior* 18(3): 292–307.

Dew, Mary A., Evelyn J. Bromet, and Lili Penkower. 1992. "Mental Health Effects of Job Loss in Women." *Psychological Medicine* 22(3): 751–764.

Eisenberg, Philip, and Paul F. Lazarsfeld. 1938. "The Psychological Effects of Unemployment." *Psychological Bulletin* 35(6): 358–390.

Ensminger, Margaret E., and David D. Celentano. 1990. "Gender Differences in the Effect of Unemployment on Psychological Distress." *Social Science and Medicine* 30(4): 469–477.

Erikson, Erik H. 1959. "Identity and the Life Cycle." *Psychological Issues* 1(1): 50–100.

Feather, Norman T. 1982. "Unemployment and Its Psychological Correlates: A Study of Depressive Symptoms, Self-Esteem, Protestant Ethic Values, Attributional Style and Apathy." *Australian Journal of Psychology* 34(3): 309–323.

Fryer, David M., and Roy L. Payne. 1986. "Being Unemployed: A Review of the Literature on the Psychological Experience of Unemployment." In *International Review of Industrial and Organizational Psychology*, Cary L. Cooper and Ivan T. Robertson, eds. Chichester, England: Wiley, pp. 235–278.

Goldberg, David P., and B. Blackwell. 1970. "Psychiatric Illness in General Practice: A Detailed Study Using a New Method of Case Identification." *British Medical Journal* 1: 439–443.

Goldsmith, Arthur H., and Jonathan R. Veum. 2002. "Wages and the Composition of Experience." *Southern Economics Journal* 69(2): 429–443.

Goldsmith, Arthur H., Jonathan R. Veum, and William Darity Jr. 1995. "Are Being Unemployed and Being Out of the Labor Force Distinct States? A

Psychological Approach." *Journal of Economic Psychology* 16(2): 275–295.

———. 1997. "Unemployment, Joblessness, Psychological Well-Being and Self-Esteem: Theory and Evidence." *Journal of Socio-Economics* 26(2): 133–158.

Harrison, Richard. 1976. "The Demoralising Experience of Prolonged Unemployment." *Department of Employment Gazette* 84(4): 339–348.

Heider, Fritz. 1958. *The Psychology of Interpersonal Relations.* New York: Wiley.

Jackson, Paul R., and Peter B. Warr. 1984. "Unemployment and Ill-Health: The Moderating Role of Duration and Age." *Psychological Medicine* 14: 605–614.

Jahoda, Marie. 1982. *Employment and Unemployment: A Social-Psychological Analysis.* New York: Cambridge University Press.

Jahoda, Marie, Paul F. Lazarsfeld, and Hans Zeisel. 1933. *Marienthal: The Sociography of an Unemployed Community* (English translation, 1971). Chicago, IL: Aldine.

Kessler, Ronald C., Peggy R. Barker, Lisa J. Colpe, Joan F. Epstein, Joseph C. Gfroerer, Eva Hiripi, Mary J. Howes, Sharon-Lise T. Normand, Ronald W. Manderscheid, Ellen E. Walters, and Alan M. Zaslavsky. 2003. "Screening for Serious Mental Illness in the General Population." *Archives of General Psychiatry* 60(2): 184–189.

Kessler, Ronald C., J. Blake Turner, and James S. House. 1989. "Unemployment, Reemployment, and Emotional Functioning in a Community Sample." *American Sociological Review* 54(4): 648–657.

McKee-Ryan, Frances M., Zhaoli Song, Connie R. Wanberg, and Angelo J. Kinicki. 2005. "Psychological and Physical Well-Being during Unemployment: A Meta-Analytic Study." *Journal of Applied Psychology* 90(1): 53–76.

Moosa, Imad A. 1997. "A Cross-Country Comparison of Okun's Coefficient." *Journal of Comparative Economics* 24(3): 335–356.

Okun, Arthur M. 1962. "Potential GNP: Its Measurement and Significance." Cowles Foundation Paper No. 190. New Haven, CT: Yale University, Cowles Foundation.

Paul, Karsten I., and Klaus Moser. 2009. "Unemployment Impairs Mental Health: Meta-Analyses." *Journal of Vocational Behavior* 74(3): 264–282.

Pearlin, Leonard, Elizabeth G. Meneghan, Morton A. Lieberman, and Joseph Mullan. 1981. "The Stress Process." *Journal of Health and Social Behavior* 22(4): 337–356.

Rosenberg, Morris. 1965. *Society and the Adolescent Self-Image.* Princeton, NJ: Princeton University Press.

Rotter, Julian B. 1966. "Generalized Expectancies for Internal versus External Control of Reinforcement." *Psychological Monographs* 80(1): 1–28.

Rowley, K. M., and Norman T. Feather. 1987. "The Impact of Unemployment in Relation to Age and Length of Unemployment." *Journal of Occupational Psychology* 60(4): 323–332.

Seligman, Martin, E. P. 1975. *Helplessness: On Depression, Development and Death*. San Francisco, CA: W. H. Freeman.

Spielberger, Charles D., Richard L. Gorsuch, Robert E. Lushene, Peter R. Vagg, and Gerard A. Jacobs. 1983. "Manual for the State–Trait Anxiety Inventory." Palo Alto, CA: Consulting Psychologists Press.

Warr, Peter B. 1987. *Work, Unemployment and Mental Health*. Oxford, United Kingdom: Oxford University Press.

Warr, Peter B., and Paul R. Jackson. 1985. "Factors Influencing the Psychological Impact of Prolonged Unemployment and Re-employment." *Psychological Medicine* 15(4): 795–807.

Weiner, Bernard. 1974. *Achievement Motivation and Attribution Theory*. Morristown, NJ: General Learning Press.

# 5

# Work Together to Let Everyone Work

## A Study of the Cooperative Job-Placement Effort in the Netherlands

Hilbrand Oldenhuis
Louis Polstra
*Centre of Applied Labour Market Research and Innovation,
Hanze University of Applied Sciences*

"We work together to let everyone work." That was the message in November 2010 when a number of employers and governmental organizations in the Netherlands publicly announced that they would cooperate with each other in order to let as many people participate in paid jobs as possible. From both an economic and a social perspective, it is clearly highly important to maximize the number of people that have paid jobs. At the end of 2008, the unemployment rate in the Netherlands was a historically low 2.7 percent. Dutch employers were having difficulties finding workers. As a result, companies were forced to cooperate with the Dutch government to fill their vacancies. However, for most employers in times of economic recession (the Dutch unemployment rate almost doubled between 2009 and 2010), decreasing the number of unemployed people will not be their highest priority.

Although on a national scale employers intend to cooperate with the government to reduce unemployment, it is not always the case for local governments. The local social services, which are responsible for local labor market policy, need information that would allow them to work more collaboratively with employers. More specifically, they wish to answer the question: Why would employers cooperate with social services by providing jobs to unemployed people via a social service agency? Two main reasons make this question a really important one to answer. First, social service agencies can use the answer in the short run to convince as many employers as possible to cooperate with them, resulting in an immediate decline in the unemployment rate. Additionally, in the long run, social services agencies that have a clear insight into employers' needs and wishes will be better able to fill the gap between supply and demand in the Dutch labor market. That is, although the unemployment rate in the Netherlands is relatively high right now and the number of vacancies is relatively low, it is expected that, due to the aging of the Dutch population (the percentage of people over 65 years of age is predicted to be 25 percent in 2030 compared with 14 percent right now), there will be an increased need for high-qualified personnel in the near future. In general, being unemployed does not make people highly qualified, but having a job does. Hence, it is important for the Dutch labor market to have as many people as possible participate in paid employment in order to avoid a large number of underqualified, long-term unemployed people while there is simultaneously a high number of unfilled vacancies. Such a situation would have devastating consequences for the whole Dutch economy. Hence, social service agencies and employers need to work together in order to let everyone work.

In this chapter, we will argue that, based on a survey we conducted with employers, the willingness of Dutch employers to cooperate with social services is highly dependent on company size. Whereas all employers underline the importance of financial considerations when it comes to their intention to cooperate with social services, employers at small companies (less than 11 employees) are especially sensitive to a more idealistic approach ("making a difference") compared to employers at middle-sized (11–100 employees) and large companies (over 100 employees).

## THEORY OF PLANNED BEHAVIOR

When it comes to determining which factors influence behavior such as cooperating with a social service, an important social psychological theory that comes to mind is the theory of planned behavior (TPB) (Ajzen 1985, 1991). In short, the theory states that the most important predictor of human (planned) behavior is the intention to behave in such a way. Applied to our subject, the TPB means that cooperating with a social service agency is primarily predicted by the intention to do so. Furthermore, this intention is predicted by three determinants. The first is the individual's attitude, that is, the global evaluation of the behavior. The second determinant, subjective norms, refers to perceived social pressure to engage in the behavior. The third determinant is perceived behavioral control: the degree to which an individual expects that he or she is capable of performing the given behavior. Especially in health psychology, the TPB has been applied to the prediction of various health-related behaviors (see Conner and Sparks [2005] for a review). But also when it comes to, for example, the prediction of traffic behavior, such as speeding (Forward 1997), dangerous passing (Parker et al. 1992), and pedestrian violations of regulations (Moyano Díaz 2002), the TPB proved to be a relatively successful framework for predicting behavior. In a meta-analytical review, Armitage and Conner (2001) report that the TPB explained an average of 39 percent of the variance in intention and 27 percent of the variance in behavior. Therefore, the TPB should be a useful theoretical framework for answering the question of which factors determine employers' willingness to cooperate with social services.

**Behavioral Beliefs**

Concerning attitudes, Ajzen (1991) states that so-called behavioral beliefs determine how positive or how negative an attitude about the given behavior will be: "Each belief links the behavior to a certain outcome, or to some other attribute such as the cost incurred by performing the behavior. Since the attributes that come to be linked to the behavior are already valued positively or negatively, we automatically and simultaneously acquire an attitude toward the behavior" (p. 191). Several beliefs concerning the outcomes of cooperating with a social service agency multiplied by their respective subjective values therefore determine how positively or how negatively an employer in general thinks about cooperating with a social service agency. Thus, we set out to determine which are the salient behavioral beliefs for employers that predict their willingness to do so.

In the preparation phase of this study, we conducted several interviews with employers, most of whom underlined the importance of financial factors. In the end, a company must stay in business, so cooperation should not cost a lot of money and time. Related to that, some employers reported that cooperation could be a convenient way to reduce a shortage of staff without having to expend too many resources. In addition, some employers mentioned the word *proud* as part of their belief system. That is, they showed a desire to make a difference. As a result, they expected to feel proud when cooperating with a social service agency to help an unemployed person to find a (new) job. Indeed, in a case study, Humphreys and Brown (2008) find that an important motive for altruistic behavior of employees of a bank is the desire to make a difference and as a result to feel proud. This is illustrated by the following quote: "You need to be proud of what you're doing, you need to be able to put your head on the pillow at night you know, thinking 'I've made a difference today,' and you need to be able to tell your Mum what you've done" (p. 408). Related to feeling proud, some employers reported that cooperation with a social service would be in line with their personal values, in terms of giving each individual a chance to climb up the societal ladder. Therefore, in our study we investigate the relative importance of each of these behavioral beliefs (money, time, reducing shortage of staff in a convenient way, pride, and the degree to which cooperation is congruent with personal values) in relation to cooperation with a social service agency.

**Subjective Norms**

Usually, subjective norms are posited as perceptions of social pressure to behave in a particular way that derive from judgments of this behavior from salient others, weighted by the motivation to comply with this pressure. For example, if an employer's friends find it really important to be socially responsible, yet the employer is not motivated to comply with the view of their friends, subjective norms will not strongly increase the intention to cooperate with social services. A few employers who were interviewed did mention important others who expressed norms compatible with cooperating with social services and indicated an associated increase in their likelihood to act similarly. Therefore, we decided to include a measure of subjective norms in our study.

**Perceived Behavioral Control**

In many studies, perceived behavioral control proved to be an important predictor of intentions and resulting behavior (e.g., Norman 2011; Askelson et al. 2010; White, Terry, and Hogg 1994). However, based on our interviews, we omitted this factor from our study. Among the employers we interviewed, we did not find any concerns that related to whether or not they believed that they would be able to perform the given behavior. That is, no employer perceived any external or internal barriers that would stand in the way of cooperating with a social service. Most of the research on perceived behavioral control deals with behavior that seems harder to perform than cooperating with a social service agency, such as exercise behavior (White, Terry, and Hogg 1994), attempts to reduce binge drinking behavior (Norman 2011), or vaccinating girls against human papillomavirus (Askelson et al. 2010). Cooperating with a social service agency is, in the eyes of the interviewed employers, under complete volitional control, whereas, in general, the aforementioned behaviors are under less volitional control.

When a given behavior is perceived to be under complete volitional control, the actor believes that he or she is able to engage in the given behavior (high perceived behavioral control). For behaviors that are under less volitional control, the extent to which individuals believe they can perform the behavior will be especially important as a predictor of the intention to act. Still, it is necessary for employers to expect that they will be able to cooperate with social services before actually intending to cooperate. However, based on our interviews, we expected that feelings of perceived behavioral control would be relatively high for all employers. Thus, unlike behavioral beliefs and subjective norms, we did not expect that perceived behavioral control would significantly contribute to the prediction of (differences in) intention to cooperate with social services. We did not want to ask our respondents relatively superfluous questions, and therefore we did not consider perceived behavioral control. However, based on the TPB, we did consider behavioral beliefs and the subjective norms concerning cooperating with a social service.

## Belief in a Just World

Another theoretical notion that could be useful in predicting employers' willingness to cooperate with social services is the "just-world hypothesis" (Lerner and Miller 1978). People with a strong belief in a just world hold a belief system that people deserve what they get and get what they deserve. It could be argued that people who strongly believe in a just world are not highly motivated to help unfortunate people (such as unemployed people) because they are likely to believe that those people themselves are to be blamed for their unfortunate position (see, for example, Hafer [2000]). On the other hand, employers with a weak belief in a just world could be more willing to help the unemployed. Thus, in our interviews, one employer mentioned his conviction that he himself could end up being unemployed just as easily as the "real" unemployed people (for example, by getting in an accident), and that this conviction was a strong motivation for him to cooperate with a social service agency. Therefore, we decided to investigate the role of this factor as it relates to predicting the intention to cooperate with social services.

## Company's Goals

The last factor we considered important deals with the concept of corporate social responsibility, which is a major issue in the world of industry and business. Many companies state their commitment to social responsibility in their official communications and have the explicit goal of being socially responsible. Hence, we investigated whether the degree to which an employer states that his or her company expresses an explicit goal related to corporate social responsibility would affect the intention to provide an unemployed person with a job via a social service agency. Specifically, we examined the role of several behavioral beliefs (those that deal with money, time, reducing shortage of staff, pride, and the expectation that it would be in line with personal values); subjective norms; the degree to which an employer believes that being unemployed only happens to people who deserve it (belief in a just world); and the company's goals in relation to corporate social responsibility. Furthermore, on an exploratory basis we investigated whether there would be differences between companies as a function of their size. It seems plausible that employers or HR-managers of large companies will have a solely "bureaucratic" viewpoint when it comes to cooperating with a social service agency. As a result, it could be that among managers or employers at large companies, there is less room to act on idealistically motivated reasons to cooperate with a social service compared to employers at smaller companies.

## METHOD

### Respondents

We sent a digital questionnaire to a total of 7,870 companies in the city of Groningen (the Netherlands) and asked that the respondents be those who were responsible for recruiting and hiring. We received 697 responses from employers (response rate = 8.8 percent). Among those, 283 were self-employed earners, and analyses showed that these employers on average do not have a high intention to cooperate with social services (1.93 on a 5-point scale) and thus we excluded them from our study. We based our results on the remaining 414 respondents. Among them there were 197 employers at small companies (2–10 employees), 156 employers at middle-sized companies (11–100 employees), and 61 employers at large companies (over 100 employees).

### Measures

The questionnaire consisted of several parts constructed to measure intention to cooperate, behavioral beliefs regarding cooperation with a social service agency, subjective norms, belief in a just world, and the company's important goals, respectively.

### Intention

The main dependent variable, intention to cooperate, was measured by a single item: "To what extent do you intend to cooperate with a social service agency within the next two years?" Respondents could answer on a 5-point scale (1 = definitely not, 5 = definitely; $M = 2.89$, $SD = 1.26$).

### Behavioral beliefs

Respondents evaluated the importance and likelihood of the following aspects of cooperating with social services: pride, congruent with personal values, financially desirable outcomes, saving time, and useful for reducing shortage of staff. First, respondents rated the importance of these aspects when it comes to deciding whether or not to cooperate with a social service agency, on a 5-point scale ranging from 1 (extremely unimportant) to 5 (extremely important). Next, respondents indicated the likelihood that cooperation with a social service agency would result in these outcomes. Scores were rated on a 5-point scale ranging from 1 (extremely unlikely) to 5 (extremely likely). Scores for each behavioral belief were computed by constructing the product of the importance and likelihood of each aspect (see Table 5.1 for an overview of the means and standard deviations for each behavioral belief).

### Subjective norms

Subjective norms were measured by computing the product of two items. On the first item the respondents were asked to rate their estimation of the opinion of important others in their social environment about cooperation with a social service agency in order to help unemployed people to reintegrate to work. Their answer could vary from 1 (extremely negative) to 5 (extremely positive). On the second item the respondents were asked to rate their motivation to comply with these others' opinions on a 5-point scale ($1 =$ not at all, $5 =$ very much; $M$ of the product of these two items $= 6.06$, $SD = 4.97$).

### Belief in a just world

To measure to what extent the respondents think that people get what they deserve when it comes to being unemployed, we constructed two items: 1) "It is not possible for someone who really wants to work to be unemployed for a long period," and 2) "Unemployed people should primarily blame themselves for their unemployment." The respondents could answer these two items by stating their level of agreement, ranging from 1 (totally disagree) to 5 (totally agree). They were combined into a single score by computing the average response on both items ($r = 0.65$, $M = 2.81$, $SD = 0.85$).

**Table 5.1  Means and Standard Deviations of Behavioral Beliefs**

|  | Mean | Standard deviation |
|---|---|---|
| Pride | 9.10 | 4.87 |
| Consistent with personal values | 11.72 | 6.00 |
| Saving money | 10.35 | 6.07 |
| Saving time | 7.42 | 5.24 |
| Reducing shortage of staff | 9.40 | 6.34 |

SOURCE: Author's calculations.

### Company's goals

Two items were constructed to measure the extent to which the company had an explicit goal of engaging in corporate social responsibility: 1) "Making money is an important goal of my company" ($M = 3.13$, $SD = 1.23$), and 2) "Expressing a social image is an important goal of my company" ($M = 2.96$, $SD = 1.09$). Respondents could answer by stating their level of agreement, ranging from 1 (totally disagree) to 5 (totally agree). These two items were unrelated, $r = -0.07$, $df = 412$, $p = 0.14$. Therefore, these two items were treated as separate variables.

The questionnaire ended with several questions regarding company size and respondents' gender and age. The latter two did not yield any significant effects concerning the intention to cooperate with a social service agency; therefore, we omit these variables from our description of the results.

### RESULTS

We divided the total number of 414 respondents into three groups based on company size. In general, the large ($N = 61$) and middle-sized companies ($N = 156$) showed the highest intention to cooperate with social services ($M = 3.28$, $SD = 1.31$ and $M = 3.06$, $SD = 1.23$ respectively). The difference between large and middle-sized companies did not reach significance. Compared to the large and middle-sized companies a post hoc test showed that small companies ($N = 197$) expressed a significantly lower intention to cooperate with social services than large and middle-sized companies: $M = 2.64$, $SD = 1.22$; highest $p < 0.01$.

We conducted three separate regression analyses (for small companies, middle-sized companies, and large companies) to detect which factors contribute to the prediction of the intention to cooperate with social services. This criterion variable was regressed on each behavioral belief separately, subjective norms, the measure concerning belief in a just world, and the company's goal (each predictor was standardized). It is possible to summarize all these behavioral beliefs into one single "global attitude" measure (see, for example, De Groot and Steg [2007]). However, in our opinion it is more interesting to explore the role of each behavioral belief separately. In so doing, we can make more clear-cut practical recommendations than if we combined these behavioral beliefs into one, more abstract global attitude measure.

Table 5.2 summarizes the regression coefficients for the small companies, middle-sized companies, and large companies. For small companies the following factors reached significance: pride, financially desirable outcomes, saving time, and subjective norms. For middle-sized companies, the only factors that reached significance were financially desirable outcomes and saving time, and for large companies it was only saving time.

To conclude, for small companies, economically driven motives such as time and money, along with more idealistically and personally driven motives such as expecting to feel proud and to be respected, contribute significantly to the prediction of the intention to cooperate with social services. For middle-sized and large companies no such factors are important. For these companies, primarily economic considerations (time and money) determine whether they are willing to cooperate with social services. Finally, no other factors, such as the belief in a just world or the degree to which it is important for a company to express a social image, reached significance for small, middle-sized, or large companies.

## DISCUSSION

Why would employers cooperate with social services by providing unemployed people with a job? The (beginning of the) answer is, "Well, that depends." It depends on the size of the company. While employ-

**Table 5.2 Regression of Intention to Cooperate with Social Services on Behavioral Beliefs, Subjective Norms, Belief in a Just World, and Company's Goals**

| | Small companies | | | | | Middle-sized companies | | | | | Large companies | | | | |
|---|---|---|---|---|---|---|---|---|---|---|---|---|---|---|---|
| | $\beta$ | $t$ | $R^2$ | $F$ | $df$ | $\beta$ | $t$ | $R^2$ | $F$ | $df$ | $\beta$ | $t$ | $R^2$ | $F$ | $df$ |
| | | | 0.25*** | 6.77 | 9,187 | | | 0.25*** | 5.43 | 9,146 | | | 0.38** | 3.36 | 9,500 |
| Pride | 0.26 | 2.72** | | | | 0.10 | 0.90 | | | | 0.09 | 0.44 | | | |
| Consistent with personal values | 0.14 | 1.74 | | | | 0.13 | 1.14 | | | | 0.19 | 1.11 | | | |
| Saving money | 0.22 | 2.58 | | | | 0.32 | 3.10** | | | | -0.16 | -1.20 | | | |
| Saving time | 0.25 | 2.91** | | | | 0.23 | 2.51* | | | | 0.49 | 3.28** | | | |
| Reducing shortage of staff | -0.11 | -1.32 | | | | 0.07 | 0.82 | | | | 0.10 | 0.77 | | | |
| Subjective norms | 0.22 | 2.87** | | | | 0.12 | 1.38 | | | | -0.05 | -0.27 | | | |
| Belief in a just world | -0.02 | -0.24 | | | | -0.12 | -1.36 | | | | -0.14 | -1.12 | | | |
| Goal: social responsibility | 0.06 | 0.80 | | | | 0.12 | 1.36 | | | | -0.15 | -1.14 | | | |
| Goal: making money | -0.13 | -1.53 | | | | 0.03 | 0.39 | | | | 0.03 | 0.25 | | | |

NOTE: *$p < 0.05$, **$p < 0.01$, and ***$p < 0.001$.
SOURCE: Authors' calculations.

ers of middle-sized and large companies primarily base their intentions on economic considerations, employers of small companies base their intentions on more idealistically and personally driven motivations. Why did we find these results? Although our study was not set up to answer this question, and more research is needed to fully explore it, we do have a suggestion: It is very conceivable that for employers of small companies there is a strong connection between their personal self and their company. If this is the case, it is not surprising that in addition to more economic considerations concerning time and money, subjective norms and expecting to feel proud are also important factors for determining the intent to cooperate with social services.

In our study, for small companies, the questionnaire was probably filled out by the owner of the company (since the owner is responsible for recruiting and hiring new staff), while for the larger companies, the questionnaire was probably filled out by a human resources manager. In the latter case, the connection between the respondent and the company is in general less strong, resulting in a less important role for idealism and personality. In addition, this line of reasoning may also account for the less important role of the behavioral belief concerning money among large companies. Since the respondents in this group are, in general, not the owners themselves, it is not their money that they spend or save by cooperating with a social service agency—more likely, it is primarily their own time that they will win or save. Hence, time for them is a more important consideration than money.

Based on the results of our study, we would advise social services in the Netherlands to take company size into account when they try to find cooperation partners. Smaller companies seem to be more sensitive to idealism and an approach based on subjective norms ("Think of how others will appreciate you!") than middle-sized and large companies. However, based on our above reasoning, it might be especially important for social services, over and above company size, to determine how strong the connection is between the person with whom they are dealing and the given company. An approach that is based more on idealism ("making a difference") is probably more effective in the case of a strong connection than when this connection is less strong. Importantly, whether the connection between the person and the company is stronger or weaker, the economic picture, especially in terms of time, should always be appealing, since for all companies economic considerations are important factors to act on when it comes to cooperating with a social service agency.

Another remarkable finding is the lack of an effect of the company's goals in our study. Whether the company has an explicit goal concerning making money and/or an explicit goal concerning being socially responsible, it does not affect the employers' intention to cooperate with a social service agency. On the one hand, it is reassuring for the social services that apparently employers perceive no discrepancy between making money and cooperating with a social service (otherwise there should have been a negative correlation between the degree to which the respondents stated that making money is an important goal of their company and the intention to cooperate). On the other hand, it is somewhat disappointing for social services that stating that your company has an explicit goal to be socially responsible does not result in a higher intention to cooperate with social services. It is possible that employers in general just do not know whether cooperating with a social service agency makes sense when they have explicit corporate social responsibility goals. However, it is also conceivable that expressing such goals primarily serves a marketing function—it gives companies the opportunity to express a positive image. More research is needed to explore whether employers in general express their company's goals in terms of corporate social responsibility primarily for marketing reasons, and to explore under what circumstances employers will and will not act on their corporate social responsibility goals by cooperating with social services.

## Theoretical Implications

During the formulation of our study, we were guided by several theoretical perspectives, the first of which was the theory of planned behavior (Ajzen 1985, 1991). Besides an attitudinal influence (based on the separate behavioral beliefs) on intention, we only found evidence for a significant influence of subjective norms among employers at small companies. We used a rather general measure of subjective norms (only based on the perceived norm of "important others") instead of measuring the norms of several reference groups. According to Armitage and Conner (2001), measuring subjective norms by means of a single item measure (which closely resembles our measure) can account for a low correlation between subjective norms and intention. However, in their meta-analysis the subjective norm-intention correlation is significantly weaker than, for example, the attitude-intention correlation. In line with Armitage and Conner, we could conclude that while "this does not present sufficient evidence to warrant discarding the construct, it does perhaps indicate that it is the part of the theory of planned behavior that most requires further study" (p. 482). To fully identify the normative component of human behavior and to increase the predictive power of the theory of planned behavior, one should probably take into account that there are many types of norms, besides subjective norms (see, for example, Cialdini, Kallgren, and Reno [1991]), which could all have profound influences on intention and behavior. In addition to that, our results show that a subjective norm is only an important factor, when the consequences of the given behavior solely shine on the actor, as was the case for the employers of the small companies in our study.

The second theoretical viewpoint we used was the notion of the "just-world hypothesis" (Lerner and Miller 1978). Believing that being unemployed is something that people deserve should lower the intention to cooperate with a social service agency. However, we did not find any evidence for this line of reasoning. Contrary to other studies, such as Fox et al. (2010) and Van den Bos and Maas (2009), we used a situation-specific measure of belief in a just world. That is, we asked respondents whether they viewed unemployment as something that unemployed people simply deserve. We did so because there is no theoretical reason to expect that a strong general belief in a just world (i.e., the belief that the world is just for people generally) should be closely related to a more situation-specific measure of belief in a just world. That is, if individuals believe that people in general get what they deserve, then it is plausible that they also believe that unemployed people get what they deserve, namely, unemployment. Yet, such a blunt measure might have led to more socially desirable answers and, as such, a less expressed belief in a just world concerning unemployed people among respondents with a strong belief in a just world.

In line with our reasoning concerning the strength of the connectedness between the respondent and the company, however, it is not inconceivable that at least for the middle-sized and the large companies, the connection between the respondent and the company was too weak to let such a personal factor affect the intention to cooperate. That does not account, however, for the absence of significant results among employers of small companies. The role of the "belief in a just world" concept therefore remains unclear when it comes to employers' intention to cooperate with social services.

## CONCLUSION

Why would employers cooperate with social service agencies by providing unemployed people with a job? The answer to this question should have far-reaching implications for the policies that social service agencies undertake to find employers that are willing to cooperate with them. When employers have difficulties finding sufficient numbers of new employees, as is the case during periods of economic boom, social service agencies do not really need to put themselves into the employer's psychological frame of reference. However, when unemployment rates are high, as is the case now, it becomes clear that these agencies need to know what is considered important by employers, who have to decide whether or not they will cooperate with them. Social service agencies that are apt to take an employer's perspective will be better able to decrease immediately the number of unemployed people. Moreover, getting to know employers' needs and wishes is especially important for Dutch social service agencies in order to be better able to reduce the expected mismatch of the Dutch labor market in the long run. Due to the aging of the population, Dutch society simply cannot afford to exclude people for a long period from the labor market.

Our results suggest that social service agencies should take company size into account. We found that employers of small companies (2–10 employees) are much more willing to cooperate with social service agencies due to idealistic motives than are employers of middle-sized (11–100 employees) and large companies (more than 100 employees). In contrast, for middle-sized and large companies, more rational factors such as (the lack of) time and money determine whether or not they are willing to cooperate with social service agencies. Hence, although most companies do officially state their social responsibility, our results show that only for small companies is cooperating with social service agencies not solely a matter of economics (although they do emphasize the importance of economic factors). In trying to persuade employers to cooperate with them, social service agencies should differentiate the rationale for their policies as a function of company size. That is, when contacting small companies, they should base their approach on economic motives such as time and money, as well as on an idealistic desire to "do the right thing" and on subjective norms, whereas with middle-sized and large companies, they should primarily adopt an approach that is based on motives such as time and money.

## References

Ajzen, Icek. 1985. "From Intentions to Action: A Theory of Planned Behavior." In *Action Control: From Cognitions to Behaviors*, Julius Kuhl and Jurgen Beckman, eds. New York: Springer, pp. 11–39.

———. 1991. "The Theory of Planned Behavior." *Organizational Behavior and Human Decision Processes* 50(2): 179–211.

Askelson, Natoshhia M., Shelly Campo, John B. Lowe, Leslie K. Dennis, Sandi Smith, and Julie Andsager. 2010. "Factors Related to Physicians' Willingness to Vaccinate Girls against HPV: The Importance of Subjective Norms and Perceived Behavioral Control." *Women & Health* 50(2): 144–158.

Armitage, Chris J., and Mark Conner. 2001. "Efficacy of the Theory of Planned Behaviour: A Meta-Analytical Review." *British Journal of Social Psychology* 40(4): 471–499.

Cialdini, Robert B., Carl A. Kallgren, and Raymond R. Reno. 1991. "A Focus Theory of Normative Conduct: A Theoretical Refinement and Reevaluation of the Role of Norms in Human Behavior." In *Advances in Experimental Social Psychology*, Vol. 24, Mark P. Zanna, ed. New York: Academic Press, pp. 201–234.

Conner, Mark, and Paul Sparks. 2005. "Theory of Planned Behaviour and Health Behaviour." In *Predicting Health Behaviour*, Mark Conner and Paul Norman, eds. New York: Open University Press, McGraw-Hill Education, pp. 170–222.

De Groot, Judith, and Linda Steg. 2007. "General Beliefs and the Theory of Planned Behavior: The Role of Environmental Concerns in the TPB." *Journal of Applied Social Psychology* 37(8): 1817–1836.

Forward, S. E. 1997. "Measuring Attitudes and Behavior Using the Theory of Planned Behavior." In *Traffic and Transport Psychology: Theory and Application*, Talib Rothengatter and E. Carbonell Vayá, eds. Amsterdam, The Netherlands: Pergamon, pp. 353–365.

Fox, Claire L., Tracey Elder, Josephine Gater, and Elizabeth Johnson. 2010. "The Association between Adolescents' Beliefs in a Just World and Their Attitudes to Victims of Bullying." *British Journal of Educational Psychology* 80(2): 183–198.

Hafer, Carolyn L. 2000. "Do Innocent Victims Threaten the Belief in a Just World? Evidence from a Modified Stroop Task." *Journal of Personality and Social Psychology* 79(2): 165–173.

Humphreys, Michael, and Andrew D. Brown. 2008. "An Analysis of Corporate Social Responsibility at Credit Line: A Narrative Approach." *Journal of Business Ethics* 80(3): 403–418.

Lerner, Melvin J., and Dale T. Miller. 1978. "Just World Research and the Attribution Process: Looking Back and Ahead." *Psychological Bulletin* 85(5): 1030–1051.

Moyano Díaz, Emilio. 2002. "Theory of Planned Behavior and Pedestrians' Intentions to Violate Traffic Regulations." *Transportation Research* (Part F) 5(3): 169–175.

Norman, Paul. 2011. "The Theory of Planned Behavior and Binge Drinking among Undergraduate Students: Assessing the Impact of Habit Strength." *Addictive Behaviors* 36(5): 502–507.

Parker, Dianne, Antony S. R. Manstead, Stephen G. Stradling, James T. Reason, and James S. Baxter. 1992. "Intention to Commit Driving Violations: An Application of the Theory of Planned Behavior." *Journal of Applied Psychology* 77(1): 94–101.

Van den Bos, Kees, and Marjolein Maas. 2009. "On the Psychology of the Belief in a Just World: Exploring Experiential and Rationalistic Paths to Victim Blaming." *Personality and Social Psychology Bulletin* 35(12): 1567–1578.

White, Katherine M., Deborah J. Terry, and Michael A. Hogg. 1994. "Safer Sex Behavior: The Role of Attitudes, Norms and Control Factors." *Journal of Applied Social Psychology* 24(24): 2164–2192.

# 6
# Stabilizing Employment

## The Role of Short-Time Compensation

Vera Brusentsev
*Swarthmore College*

Wayne Vroman
*Urban Institute*

One response to the Great Recession of 2008–2009 in several economies of the Organisation of Economic Co-operation and Development (OECD) was increased reliance on short-time compensation (STC) and other work-sharing arrangements that temporarily reduce weekly hours to ease labor market dislocations and to avoid the personal and economic costs of elevated levels of long-term unemployment. Short-time compensation has been credited with helping to stabilize employment in the face of sharp reductions in real gross domestic product (GDP). The research conducted by Burda and Hunt (2011) and Boeri and Bruecker (2011) concludes that the STC program in Germany (*Kurzarbeit*) was a major contributor in stabilizing German employment in 2009 and 2010.

As labor markets in the United States recover from the Great Recession, it is appropriate to assess the performance of the economy during this period and consider ways of structuring labor market institutions to lessen the economic hardships of future recessions. Not only did U.S. product markets deteriorate, but labor markets also experienced sharp decreases in employment, steep increases in unemployment, and record high levels of long-term unemployment. Given the severity of labor market conditions since 2007, this chapter examines the recent performance of STC in states with such programs and assesses their impact on employment. The chapter begins with an introduction to STC and a description of some of the important features of the program, and then reviews the performance of STC in the United States for the

17 states that have operated programs for several years. The next section reviews foreign experience with STC, with particular attention to the performance of STC programs in Canada, Germany, and Belgium. The following section discusses ways to increase STC usage in the United States. While some suggestions are obvious, others would make changes in the way STC plans currently function within state unemployment insurance (UI) programs.

The chapter reaches three main conclusions. First, STC has the potential to prevent layoffs and stabilize employment in short-run cyclical fluctuations. While program usage increases sharply at the start of a recession, the increased utilization lasts for a comparatively short period. Second, the programs in the United States are small in scale and do not meaningfully affect labor market adjustments at the macro level. Third, if STC were to play a larger role during the economic recovery as well as a larger role in future recessions, the programs would need to be enlarged and the pace of adoptions expanded. In addition to presenting suggestions for increasing STC usage, the chapter assesses the February 2012 legislation: the Middle Class Tax Relief and Job Creation Act of 2012 (PL12-96).

## AN OVERVIEW OF WORK SHARING

Short-time compensation work-sharing programs, now present in many economies, are intended to reduce the volume of layoffs during periods of slack labor demand.[1] Rather than reducing hours by laying off (nonprejudicial separations) some workers, a wider pool of workers at the workplace is retained but at reduced weekly hours of work. For example, to reduce hours by 20 percent in a work unit that employs 100 persons working 40-hour weeks, there would need to be 20 layoffs. Alternatively, all 100 in the work unit could be placed on 32-hour schedules. Both measures would reduce hours by 20 percent.

These employment retention programs provide partial unemployment compensation (UC) benefits to workers placed on shorter schedules. For example, if UC benefits replace half of previous weekly wages, then someone on a 32-hour schedule would receive 80 percent of their full weekly wages and partial UC benefits equal to 10 percent of weekly wages. Thus, part of the reduction in income caused by the reduction in hours is offset by partial UC benefits. In this simple example, participants in STC would receive take-home pay equal to 90 percent of their full weekly wages.[2]

In the United States in 2011, 21 states had STC programs that were generally small in scale. While 4 states introduced STC programs during 2010 and 2011, the other 17 states have operated these programs for 20 years or longer. A program for STC is established through legislation as part of a state's UI law. Short-time compensation plans, administered as part of UI, are initiated when an employer files an application with the UI agency. To be eligible to participate in STC, the employer must be experience rated, not delinquent in paying UI taxes, and explain the reason(s) for needing to adjust work hours. Plans submitted to the UI agency are often approved within one or two weeks.

Short-time compensation plans need to conform to state requirements regarding a minimum percentage reduction in hours at the affected work unit, plan duration, the minimum and maximum reduction in hours for affected workers, and the maximum number of weeks STC benefits will be paid. Table 6A.1 in Appendix 6A displays important state-level requirements for 17 states with long-standing STC programs. Plans generally last 25 or 52 weeks and maximum payable weeks are usually 26 or 52. For affected workers, the reduction in hours is bounded between a minimum (10–20 percent in all states) and a maximum (40–50 percent in nearly all states). Plans also must specify the treatment of fringe benefits (usually either full maintenance or reduced by the proportionate reduction in hours worked). When workers are unionized, the plan must be approved by the collective bargaining unit.

Certain features of STC are linked to standard UI provisions. One is that the benefits paid to participants count against the experience-rated UI taxes paid by the employer. Since the employer initiates this reduction in hours, STC payments are experience rated in the same way as a layoff. When claimants start to collect STC, the payments count against their maximum potential payment for the benefit year (the 12-month period for which current UI eligibility applies). For example, someone otherwise eligible for 26 weeks of benefits under full unemployment would only be eligible for 24 weeks if they collected STC one day per week for 10 weeks earlier in the same benefit year. Most states make regular recipients serve a waiting week before collecting benefits. For

STC recipients, this requirement means they can start collecting in the second week of the STC claim. While regular UI recipients are required to search for work, this requirement is waived for STC recipients since they remain employed.

## EMPIRICAL ANALYSIS OF STC IN THE UNITED STATES

The STC reporting system generates monthly data that can be compared with regular state UI data. Initial claims, first payments, weeks claimed, weeks compensated, exhaustions and total benefit payments are routinely reported, along with equivalent initial claims and equivalent weeks claimed. In the latter two series, claims are converted to equivalent full weeks; that is, a week claimed by five persons working under a 20 percent reduction in weekly hours represents one equivalent week claimed. Under certain assumptions, the equivalent weeks claimed show the number of layoffs and weeks of full unemployment avoided by the use of STC.

The empirical analysis focuses on STC equivalent weeks claimed measured as a percentage of regular UI weeks claimed in annual data for the past three business cycles. For 13 of 17 states, the data extend from 1989 to 2010; there are fewer years in four states.[3] All regression equations use the same specification: the equivalent-weeks-claimed percentage is explained by the total unemployment rate (TUR) in the state and a linear trend. The TUR is entered for both the current year and the previous year. Both the current TUR and the lagged TUR coefficients show how equivalent weeks claimed behave relative to regular weeks claimed. A positive coefficient for the TUR indicates that STC equivalent weeks increase more rapidly than regular weeks in a recession when the TUR increases.

Table 6.1 summarizes the 17 regression equations by showing the distribution of the signs and statistical significance of the coefficients. Table 6B.1 in Appendix 6B displays the full regression results. All 17 coefficients for the current TUR are positive and statistically significant. A remarkably consistent pattern is present in all 17 states: when unemployment increases, STC equivalent weeks increase more rapidly than regular UI weeks claimed.

**Table 6.1  Coefficients from STC Regressions, 1989–2010**

|  | Positive, significant | Positive, not significant | Negative, not significant | Negative, significant | Total |
|---|---|---|---|---|---|
| Constant | 1 | 4 | 4 | 8 | 17 |
| State unemp. rate—TUR% | 17 | 0 | 0 | 0 | 17 |
| State TUR% lagged | 0 | 0 | 4 | 13 | 17 |
| Linear trend | 9 | 5 | 1 | 2 | 17 |

SOURCE: Regression equations displayed in Table 6B.1 of Appendix 6B.

The effect of the lagged TUR is also consistent. All 17 slope coefficients are negative and 13 are statistically significant: equivalent weeks of STC decline relative to regular weeks in the second year of a recessionary period. As the economy travels further through a recession, the volume of STC claims decreases even though unemployment may remain high or even increase. Comparing the absolute size of the two sets of coefficients, those for the lagged TUR are generally from half to fully equal to the current TUR coefficients. Not only is there a falloff, but the falloff is also large relative to the increase in the first year of the recession.

The linear trend coefficients in Table 6.1 present a more mixed picture.[4] For 14 of the 17 states there is an upward (positive) trend in STC usage with nine trends statistically significant. Three states exhibit a negative trend, and in two of them the trend is statistically significant (Florida and Maryland). Despite the predominance of positive trends, STC programs are, and remain, small in all states. Note in Table 6B.1 of Appendix 6B that the STC equivalent-weeks percentage exceeds 1.0 percent in just one state (Rhode Island) for the full data period; the percentage exceeds 0.4 in just four other states for the same period (California, Kansas, Missouri, and Vermont).

The underlying data illustrate not only the unusual severity of the Great Recession but also its effect on the scale of STC usage. Over the 22 years from 1989 to 2010, the highest equivalent-weeks-claimed percentage occurred in 2009 for 16 of the 17 states (all but Kansas).

Even though the TUR was higher in 2010 than in 2009 in most of the 17 states, the equivalent-weeks-claimed percentage in 2010 fell below the 2009 percentage in all but one state (Washington).

The regression results shown in Table 6B.1 and summarized in Table 6.1 portray a remarkably consistent pattern. When the economy enters a recession, STC usage increases sharply and much more rapidly than regular UI claims. Usage then falls, however, even in the face of continued high unemployment. The interpretation of the regression results seems obvious. Going into a recession, employers establish STC plans and place workers on reduced weekly schedules. These workers, however, do not remain on short schedules for very long. As the recession lengthens they exit through two outflows. While some workers return to full weekly work schedules, others experience full layoffs. For the latter group, STC delays the onset of full unemployment. For participating employers, STC provides more time to observe the depth and duration of the downturn and yields improved information upon which to make better informed adjustments in staffing.

For firms that retain long-run viability, there are two important advantages in utilizing STC programs: 1) the increased level of worker retention, and 2) reduced training costs since fewer new hires are needed in the ensuing upturn. For workers, there are fewer layoffs early in the recession and a different pattern of burden sharing (wider but smaller per-person losses for affected workers) due to reduced layoffs. One disadvantage for workers who eventually do lose their jobs is that STC only delays the layoffs—it is not avoided. For them STC has simply delayed the timing of the job loss.[5]

Some other aspects of worker experiences with STC can be inferred from state reports. Because the states report both weeks claimed and equivalent weeks claimed, the size of the reductions in weekly schedules can be ascertained. The higher the ratio of equivalent weeks to total weeks, the larger the reduction in work schedules; for example, a ratio of 0.20 suggests a reduction of one day from a five-day week. Overall, the reductions in work schedules have generally been modest. For 14 states, the equivalent weeks to weeks ratio between 2000 and 2010 averaged between 0.176 and 0.265. Ratios in this range suggest that reductions for STC participants usually averaged one to one-and-one-half days per week. These ratios also indicate that the number of individuals participating in STC is 3–5 times larger than suggested by the equivalent weeks ratios examined in the regressions.

As with temporary layoff unemployment, participation in STC is generally short term. Between 2000 and 2010, the mean duration of STC was shorter than for regular UI benefits in 13 of the 14 states with reliable STC duration data.[6] The ratio of the two averages was below 0.80 in 10 states, and only in Rhode Island and Vermont were they similar in size. Moreover, exhaustion of benefits while on STC is rare because duration is short and a compensated week usually involves only one or two days in benefit status. Exhaustion rates between 2000 and 2010 were significantly lower for persons receiving first payments under STC compared to the regular UI program in 15 of the 17 states with STC programs. The average exhaustion rate for these 11 years was almost always less than 5 percent for STC recipients compared to 30 percent or higher for regular UI program recipients.

One would expect STC recipients to have higher wages and, hence, higher weekly benefits than those on layoff and other job losers because a layoff typically affects less senior workers. The STC data support this expectation. In the 13 states where full weekly benefits for STC recipients can be calculated, their average STC benefits consistently exceeded average weekly benefits in the regular UI program. The ratio of the STC average to the regular program average during the 2000–2010 period ranged between 1.00 and 1.15 for 10 of the 13 states. Since the reported data do not identify the occupations of STC participants, we cannot compare the skill levels of participants to regular UI recipients.

Three concluding comments are appropriate as a summary of the empirical work in this section of the chapter. First, utilization of STC was very sensitive to the business cycle over the last three recessions for which reported data are available. Second, the utilization of STC was highest during the early stages of the Great Recession. Third, the scale of STC utilization has been consistently small in all 17 states. This last comment provides a logical connection to the next section of the chapter, which examines international experience with STC and provides a brief description of STC programs in three other advanced countries.

## COMPARISONS OF STC IN FOUR COUNTRIES

Short-time compensation work-sharing programs are present in the majority of advanced economies with new adoptions occurring in several after the onset of the Great Recession. Hijzen and Venn (2011) note that 22 OECD economies reported either introducing new measures or making adjustments to existing programs in response to the most recent downturn. Program details vary widely across countries. Here we briefly examine three foreign programs: 1) Canada, 2) Germany, and 3) Belgium. The choice of these countries is based on past experiences of the authors and knowledge of their differing scales. While all three foreign programs are larger than STC in the United States, the Canadian program can be described as similar in size. The programs in Germany and Belgium have a much larger presence in their respective labor markets. We recently reviewed the Canadian program, while the German and Belgian programs were the subject of comparative analysis in the early 1990s (Vroman 1992).

Cyclical adjustments in hours worked occur at two margins, the extensive and intensive margins, or as changes in employment and changes in hours per employed person. Germany and Belgium have extensive safety nets for employed workers that include other measures besides STC, which also facilitate adjustments in hours per employee. Prominent among these other features are working-time accounts (present in both Germany and Belgium), working-time corridors (Germany), and career interruption benefits (Belgium). Burda and Hunt (2011) and Boeri and Bruecker (2011) conclude that working-time accounts, along with STC, have played an important part in stabilizing German employment in 2009–2010. While we focus on STC, readers are reminded that other factors can influence adjustments on the intensive margin. These other factors are part of a broad framework of labor market "flexicurity" present in many OECD economies (see Chapter 2 in this volume). Because flexicurity provisions are generally not present in the United States, we merely note their relevance to the analysis of STC in other countries.

## Canada

Canada has supported an STC program since the early 1980s. While it has been comparatively small in scale, it operates in all provinces of the country and exhibits strong cyclical sensitivity. Interested employers file STC plans with the Employment Insurance (EI) agency, and claimants receive partial EI benefits under approved plans.[7] Claimants must be monetarily eligible under the same requirements as regular EI claimants. Unlike claimants for regular EI benefits, who are subject to a two-week waiting period, STC recipients are paid during the first week of eligibility. The STC payments received do not reduce future EI entitlement if the claimant subsequently becomes fully unemployed through a layoff.

With the onset of the Great Recession, Canada modified STC to broaden the scope of the program. Potential benefit duration was increased in early 2009 from 38 to 52 weeks and then to 78 weeks. Employer participation was encouraged through advertisements in the media and revised program requirements that broadened coverage and eased the application process. One change was the temporary waiver of a detailed plan to return to full work schedules. During 2009 participation in STC was the highest in the history of the Canadian program.

## Germany

Short-time compensation has been present in Germany since the end of the nineteenth century and widely used since the late 1920s. During the Great Recession the STC program, termed *Kurzarbeit*, expanded dramatically from 50,000 participants in September 2008 to 1.46 million in May 2009. Over the same period the number of participating employers increased from 1,491 to 14,936. The large increase in participation reflects the increased usage of the program by large establishments.

The STC program in Germany has a number of key features. Plans can be established if there is a "significant loss of work," the definition of which was eased in February 2009 to broaden the scope of potential STC use. The initiative to establish an STC plan can originate from the employer or from worker representatives, and both must agree on the details of the plan if workers are unionized. In nonrecessionary periods,

STC plans usually last six months, but extensions to 12 months are common. During the Great Recession, the maximum duration increased to 18 months in January 2009 and to 24 months in June. Maximum duration throughout 2010 was 18 months.

After the establishment of an STC plan, payments are administered by the employer through the company's payroll system with reimbursement to the employer from the German administrative agency, *Bundesanstalt für Arbeit* (BA). Employers are required to maintain fringe benefit contributions (for health insurance and retirement) so that employer fringe benefit costs increase for their STC workers.

Utilization of STC during the Great Recession was high, and several researchers have credited STC with the maintenance of employment during 2009 and 2010 (Boeri and Bruecker 2011; Burda and Hunt 2011; Crimmann, Wießner, and Bellmann 2010). The authors conclude that absent STC, the level of unemployment in 2009 would have been 250,000–400,000 higher in Germany.

Other factors have also contributed to the so-called German employment miracle of 2009–2010. Working-time accounts were widely used. These accounts accumulate balances when workers log overtime and, rather than receiving take-home pay immediately, the overtime pay is deposited into the accounts. Workers can then withdraw from these accounts at a later time when weekly hours are reduced. While these accounts have existed for more than 20 years and accumulated substantial balances, they were reduced by large withdrawals during 2009 and 2010. Both Boeri and Bruecker (2011) and Burda and Hunt (2011) attribute the large employment-stabilizing effects in Germany during the Great Recession to the utilization of these accounts.

The list of other factors operative in Germany also includes deliberate employer decisions to forgo overtime hours in favor of employment-stabilizing adjustments to total hours. Of some importance are working-time "corridors," which employers can use to shorten the weekly hours of less senior workers. In sum, several factors contributed to the stabilization of employment and unemployment in the face of large reductions in real output in Germany. While STC was important, other factors also played a major role in stabilizing employment and unemployment (see Chapter 2 in this volume).

## Belgium

Belgium operates an STC program of substantial size. Between 2007 and 2009 the number of beneficiaries of *chomeurs temporaires* (temporary unemployment schemes) doubled, restraining the increase in open unemployment. The program was expanded during 2009 and 2010 by increasing potential benefit duration and expanding the occupational coverage to white-collar workers.

Two other programs in Belgium pay benefits to part-time workers. Career interruption benefits are paid to those who reduce hours to pursue non–labor market activities, such as child rearing. Interruptions are temporary and may be either total or partial. Credit time accounts, first initiated in 2002, is a much smaller program than the working-time accounts in Germany, and participation did not expand much in 2009–2010. Thus in Belgium, the stabilization of employment and unemployment was attributable mainly to the program of *chomeurs temporaires.*

Table 6.2 displays comparative data on STC for the United States, Canada, Germany, and Belgium. The table has annual data for the four years from 2007 to 2010. For the United States, the data pertain to the 17 states with STC at the end of 2009. This total includes the four largest states, and the 17 states combined represent about half of the labor force and unemployment.[8] Note that for Canada and Germany certain data have been inferred. Total unemployment for all four countries is based on own-country labor force surveys.

Four aspects of Table 6.2 warrant comments. First, the table reinforces the point made in the previous section that the scale of STC in the United States is small. Even restricting the data to the 17 states with long-standing STC programs, the size in 2009, the year of highest utilization, is only 1.1 percent of regular UI recipients. Second, the strong cyclicality of STC utilization in all four economies is evident. The falloff in utilization during 2010 relative to 2009 is obvious, with the German STC percentage (column [6]) falling to half of the 2009 percentage. As stated previously, STC is utilized most intensively in the early stages of a recession. If the program is to perform a useful stabilization function, it has to be established prior to the recession, not after it has begun. Furthermore, in this slow recovery from the recession, reducing layoffs can make an important contribution to improving the labor market. Data collected by the Bureau of Labor Statistics through its Job

**Table 6.2  Comparisons of STC Programs in Four Countries, 2007–2010**

| | Total unemploy-ment (1) | Regular UC recipients (2) | STC bene-ficiaries (3) | STC equivalent bene-ficiaries (4) | Equiv. ben./ STC ben. (4)/(3) (5) | Equiv. ben./ regular ben. (%) (4)/(2) (6) |
|---|---|---|---|---|---|---|
| United States[a] | | | | | | |
| 2007 | 3,495 | 1,060 | 12.0 | 3.2 | 0.267 | 0.303 |
| 2008 | 4,531 | 1,396 | 22.6 | 6.2 | 0.275 | 0.445 |
| 2009 | 7,123 | 2,454 | 104.0 | 27.7 | 0.266 | 1.127 |
| 2010 | 7,608 | 1,954 | 67.7 | 16.8 | 0.249 | 0.862 |
| Canada | | | | | | |
| 2007 | 1,079 | 479 | 2.6 | 0.7 | 0.286[b] | 0.152 |
| 2008 | 1,117 | 486 | 4.8 | 1.4 | 0.286[b] | 0.280 |
| 2009 | 1,516 | 734 | 48.3 | 13.8 | 0.286[b] | 1.884 |
| 2010 | 1,484 | 683 | 30.9 | 8.9 | 0.286[b] | 1.296 |
| Germany | | | | | | |
| 2007 | 3,601 | 1,080 | 68.0 | 36.0 | 0.528 | 3.337 |
| 2008 | 3,141 | 917 | 102.0 | 46.0 | 0.451 | 4.994 |
| 2009 | 3,227 | 1,141 | 1,139.0 | 372.0 | 0.326 | 32.603 |
| 2010 | 2,936 | 1,027 | 535.0[c] | 174.0[c] | 0.326[c] | 16.999 |
| Belgium | | | | | | |
| 2007 | 353 | 429 | 115.0 | 30.1 | 0.261 | 6.983 |
| 2008 | 334 | 404 | 134.7 | 32.4 | 0.240 | 8.018 |
| 2009 | 380 | 434 | 210.9 | 60.6 | 0.287 | 13.951 |
| 2010 | 408 | 438 | 173.3 | 49.8 | 0.287 | 11.353 |

[a]17 states with STC in 2009.
[b]Ratio assumed by the authors based on fiscal year data from 1991–2009.
[c]Based on part-year data.
SOURCE: Data developed by the authors from national sources. Data in columns (1)–(4) are in thousands.

Openings and Labor Turnover Survey (JOLTS) indicate that even now, 22 months into the recovery, 1.8 million jobs are lost each month due to involuntary separations. Greater use of STC could further reduce these involuntary separations—resulting in a net increase of jobs—or apparent job growth.

Third, the most obvious feature of Table 6.2 is the much larger scale of the STC programs in Germany and Belgium. Column (6) shows equivalent beneficiaries as a percentage of regular UC beneficiaries: the averages during 2009 and 2010 are about 25 percent in Germany and 12 percent in Belgium. The corresponding two-year averages in the United States and Canada were 1.0 and 1.6 percent. Fourth, note the extent of the reductions from full schedules suggested by column (5): the ratio of full equivalent STC beneficiaries to the weekly/monthly numbers of STC beneficiaries. For the United States and Belgium, the proportions consistently fall between 0.25 and 0.30, whereas for Germany they show a sharp decrease in 2009–2010. In Germany the reduction in weekly schedules was about half in 2007–2008 but about one-third in 2009–2010. The average number of recipients in STC grew much more rapidly than the number of full equivalent STC recipients in 2009–2010.

A final observation about the information in Table 6.2 is the scale of the increase in unemployment in the United States compared to the other three countries. Unemployment in 2010 was more than twice its level of 2007—7.608 million versus 3.495 million.[9] The next largest increase was in Canada, roughly 50 percent. The increase in Belgium was less than 20 percent, while German unemployment did not increase in 2009–2010 despite a sharp falloff in real GDP, especially in 2009. These data merely reinforce the widely understood point that German workers fared comparatively well during the Great Recession.

## OPTIONS FOR INCREASING STC UTILIZATION IN THE UNITED STATES

We believe STC needs to be more widely utilized in the United States on both equity and efficiency grounds. Equity is promoted by sharing the burden of adjustment more equally across the workforce, and efficiency is advanced by preventing temporary factors from destroying valuable job matches (OECD 2010).

We find two aspects of STC particularly attractive when compared to the adjustments in hours worked accomplished through layoffs. First, we think STC provides a better pattern of burden sharing among workers. A wider pool is affected under STC but the reduction in income among affected persons is smaller than under layoffs. Not only does STC reduce the volume of worker dislocation but also the adjustment problems of dislocated workers, such as long spells of unemployment, reduced reemployment wage rates, and loss of health insurance and other fringe benefits. In the language of labor economics, STC shifts the locus of changes in hours worked from the extensive margin (layoffs) to the intensive margin (hours per worker). Second, training costs are reduced because workers remain employed and many return to full-time schedules at their jobs when sales and production recover to pre-recession levels.

Based on this judgment, we suggest four specific actions to increase STC utilization:

1) Disseminate information about STC and its advantages to employers and workers. While dissemination of timely information can be accomplished by various means, the following are obvious: advertise in the media, especially during the earliest stages of a recession; include information in UI tax notices to employers; and provide information to employers and workers in mass-layoff situations. The latter can be activated by the advance notice requirements of WARN legislation that requires employers with 50 or more employees to give notice 60 days prior to a planned mass layoff. State labor departments then send rapid response teams to the worksite to help plan for the subsequent developments. Rapid response teams include UI specialists who can inform employers and workers about STC and potentially influence the type of adjustments to be made.

Rhode Island, the state with the largest STC program (relative to the state labor market), has experience with avoiding plant closings when employers and workers have been informed about the STC program. This experience at plant sites has helped save jobs that eventually returned to full schedules when company sales rebounded.

2) Because of the uncertainty surrounding employer staffing decisions at the early stages of a downturn, STC plans must be comparatively easy to implement. At present, the employer must submit the STC plan to the UI agency to start the process. An alternative approach would be to let the employer initiate the STC plan, commence it immediately and administer payments within their existing payroll system, but inform the UI agency at the same time. Partial UI benefits can be paid by the employer, who is then reimbursed by the agency.[10] Under this arrangement workers would not need to apply for benefits as they are automatically enrolled and paid.[11] To ensure that plans adhere to statutory and administrative guidelines, the UI agency can audit some

plans and respond to complaints. This approach would resemble the one followed in Germany. The advantage is that it would have a rapid start-up and, more than likely, higher worker participation than at present where take-up is far from universal in STC work units.[12]

If a state deemed this approach inappropriate, an alternative would be to ease the application procedure and expedite the approval of STC applications during a recession. The UI agency would acknowledge the importance of STC by having internal administrative procedures making it of equal importance to timely payments for fully unemployed claimants.

3) A salient feature of UI in the United States is experience rating. Higher payments to laid-off employees cause future employer UI payroll taxes to increase. Experience rating is imperfect, and on average only about 60 percent of benefit payments are charged to the former employers. Situations that escape experience rating include payments that follow quits, benefits to workers when firms cease operations, and payments by employers taxed at the maximum tax rate. These payments are termed *noncharged* and *ineffectively charged* benefits. They are typically financed by a common tax, where all employers pay the same tax rate.

The payment of STC benefits could be treated as a category of noncharged benefits. In effect, the cost of STC benefits would be spread to all covered employers rather than assigned to STC employers. This procedure would provide an explicit reward for maintaining employment and reducing the volume of layoffs. In other words, STC employers would be rewarded for making adjustments at the intensive margin rather than the extensive margin. If some STC participants were subsequently severed, the later payments for full unemployment would be treated the same as other charged benefits.

4) A second aspect of STC benefit payments could also be treated differentially from regular UI benefits. When a claimant files for regular benefits and is deemed eligible, a benefit year is established. The benefit year is a 52-week period within which the claimant can collect a maximum total amount of UI benefits. For most claimants (roughly 80 percent) this amount (the maximum benefit amount [MBA]) is limited to 26 times their weekly benefit. Any payments within an established benefit year reduce the available balance from their MBA. When the remaining balance reaches zero the claimant is said to have exhausted

their claim for that year. Currently STC payments reduce the MBA remaining balance in the same way as full weekly benefits, just at a slower weekly rate that reflects the reduction from the full work schedule. Someone otherwise eligible for 26 weeks who collects STC for 10 days would only be eligible for 24 weeks of full UI benefits in the same benefit year.

This aspect of eligibility treats STC claimants like fully unemployed claimants even though they have remained employed. To the extent that STC-eligible persons are concerned about becoming fully unemployed, this treatment of their remaining MBA would inhibit their participation in STC. The United States is the only country where drawing STC benefits reduces potential benefits for full unemployment. In effect, we treat the STC participants as unemployed while other STC programs treat participants as employed. Worker participation in STC would be encouraged if STC payments did not reduce the remaining balance in the MBA.

Administration of this changed treatment would require states to separately record STC benefits and delay establishing a new benefit year when STC would otherwise be the first payment of a new benefit year. A simple way to accomplish this would be to have the federal partner fully finance STC benefit payments. This financial arrangement would involve reimbursing state UI agencies directly for STC payments. Employers in states with STC would avoid associated UI taxes altogether (including some socialized charges if STC benefits were treated as noncharged items).

Throughout its 30-year history in the United States, STC has been a small program, even in the states with STC. Implementing the four suggested changes would increase STC utilization, making it available to a wider set of workers than at present. In unionized situations there would need to be agreement by the union as to the plan's details.

Senator Jack Reed of Rhode Island has tried to foster increased use of STC and introduced STC legislation in 2010 and in 2011 with Senators Richard Durbin and Sherrod Brown (S.386.IS—Unemployment Insurance Solvency Act of 2011). Most provisions of their bill were included in the Middle Class Tax Relief and Job Creation Act of 2012 (PL12-96). The legislation includes three categories of provisions: 1) temporary federal financing of STC benefits, 2) grants to states for STC-related purposes, and 3) increased federal responsibilities for promoting STC.

The first provision of the legislation relates to temporary federal financing of STC programs. This provision not only rewards states that have existing programs, but also encourages other states to adopt STC. For states with existing programs, 100 percent of the cost of STC benefits is paid by the federal partner for three full years. States that introduce STC programs will have 50 percent of the cost of benefits subsidized for three years.

The second provision authorizes $100 million in grants to states for STC-related purposes. Grants will be disbursed for two types of activities: 1) implementing newly enacted STC programs and improving administration, and 2) promoting and enrolling employers in STC programs. The allocation formula for disbursing these grants to the states is one-third for the first activity and two-thirds for the second.

The third provision relates to increased federal and state responsibilities for promoting STC. Three new areas of responsibilities are added to the authority of the U.S. Department of Labor. First, new model language for STC legislation in the states will be prepared, updating legislative language drafted some 25 years ago. Second, technical assistance and guidance will be provided to the states in establishing and administering STC. The third establishes the requirements for reporting STC activities, a small extension to the existing reporting requirements.

Compared to the suggestions we have proposed above, the 2012 legislation includes substantial direct financial support both for STC benefit payments and for STC benefits administration. It also provides financial rewards for effective outreach to employers, whereas we rely more on information dissemination through various channels to reach employers and increase utilization. The legislation does not speak to the treatment of STC benefit charges in affecting employer UI tax rates or the treatment of the STC usage in reducing the claimant's remaining MBA. To the extent that money talks, the financial carrots of the legislation could encourage adoptions by states. While we have emphasized the role of STC at the start of a recession, it could also provide a useful role during the recovery phase of the business cycle. During the recovery phase, however, STC would play a smaller role because the volume of layoffs is much lower.

# Notes

1. The term *work sharing* as used here means reducing hours for the purpose of preserving overall employment. It does not refer to, say, two people sharing a single full-time job with each working part time.
2. Personal taxes are not considered in this example.
3. For Connecticut, Iowa, Minnesota, and Rhode Island the first year is either 1991 or 1992.
4. The linear trend variable is equal to 1 in 1989 and increases by increments of 1 in subsequent years. This variable is needed to control for slowly evolving trends. An upward trend could reflect slowly increasing awareness of STC by employers and/or workers.
5. With an STC program in place, one can expect fewer layoffs and a reduction in the economic costs associated with a job separation. It is also possible that receipt of STC acts as a signal to modify behavior and adapt to changed economic circumstances; for example, increase the rate of saving.
6. Duration for regular UI benefits and for STC is measured as the ratio of weeks compensated to first payments.
7. The UI program in Canada is called *Employment Insurance*. Monetary eligibility is based on hours of work in the past year. The minimum hours requirement varies from 420 to 700 depending upon the provincial unemployment rate.
8. The total unemployment of 7.608 million in 2010 was 51 percent of the national total of 14.825 million.
9. The national numbers for the two periods were 14.815 million versus 7.078 million, an increase of 109 percent.
10. In unionized situations there would have to be agreement by the union as to the plan's details.
11. Certain states in the Southeast, for example, the Carolinas and Georgia, already have employer-filed UI claims.
12. This aspect of STC is one finding of the Berkeley Planning Associates 1997 study of STC programs.

# Appendix 6A

# State STC Provisions in 2010

Table 6A.1 displays four key requirements that STC plans must satisfy to be approved by the UI agency. The table covers the 17 states where STC plans were operative at the end of 2009. As noted in the text, three more states created STC programs in 2010 and one in 2011.

**Table 6A.1 State STC Plan Requirements in 2010**

|  | Plan approval period (weeks) | Maximum STC weeks payable | Minimum reduction in hours (%) | Maximum reduction in hours (%) |
|---|---|---|---|---|
| Arizona | 52 | 26[a] | 10 | 40 |
| Arkansas | 52 | 26 | 10 | 40 |
| California | 26 | b | 10 | |
| Connecticut | 26 | 26[c] | 20 | 40 |
| Florida | 52 | 25 | 10 | 40 |
| Iowa | 104 | 52 | 20 | 50 |
| Kansas | 52 | 26 | 20 | 40 |
| Maryland | 26 | 26 | 10 | 50 |
| Massachusetts | 25 | 26 | 10 | 60 |
| Minnesota | 52 | 52 | 20 | 40 |
| Missouri | 52 | 26 | 20 | 40 |
| New York | | 20 | 20 | 60 |
| Oregon | 52 | 52 | 20 | 40 |
| Rhode Island | 52 | 52 | 10 | 50 |
| Texas | 52 | 52 | 10 | 40 |
| Vermont | 26 | 26 | 20 | 50 |
| Washington | 52 | 52 | 10 | 50 |

[a]Longer limit if the state-insured unemployment rate exceeds 4.0 percent of covered employment.
[b]No limit on weeks but payments cannot exceed 26 times the weekly benefit amount (WBA).
[c]26-week extension possible.
SOURCE: USDOL (2010).

# Appendix 6B

# Regression Analysis of STC Utilization in 17 States

Table 6B.1 displays results for 17 state-level regression equations typically spanning the years 1989–2010. The dependent variable is annual STC equivalent weeks claimed measured as a percentage of annual weeks in the regular UI program of each state. Each regression equation has three explanatory variables: 1) the current year's state total unemployment rate (TUR), 2) the TUR lagged one year, and 3) a linear time trend that starts in 1989. Adjacent to each estimated slope coefficient is the absolute value of its $t$-ratio. The summary measures on the right-hand side of Table 6B.1 are the adjusted $R^2$s, the standard error of estimate, and the Durbin-Watson statistic (DW). The final columns display the mean of the dependent variable and the maximum percentage. The table also identifies four states where STC data were not available from 1989 due to later start dates for the programs (1991 for Iowa and Rhode Island; 1992 for Connecticut and Minnesota).

For most states the fits are quite satisfactory, with adjusted $R^2$s of at least 0.50 for 13 states and standard errors below 0.30 for 15 states. The generally small scale of STC is vividly illustrated by the small means in the right-hand column of Table 6B.1. Rhode Island is the only state where the mean over the full period exceeds 1.0 percent of regular UI claims. Only four other states have means that exceed 0.40 (California, Kansas, Missouri, and Vermont). The small scale of STC is also illustrated by the maximum annual percentages during the estimation period. While most exceed 1.0 percent, only two maxima exceed 2.0 percent, Kansas and Rhode Island at 3.24 and 4.17 percent, respectively.

While the summary measures in Table 6B.1 show the small scale of STC, the regression results point to a pattern of strong cyclical sensitivity. All 17 slope coefficients on the current year TUR are positive and their $t$-ratios all exceed 2.0, the threshold for statistical significance. The $t$-ratios in eight states even exceed 5.0; the slopes are highly significant. When unemployment increases, utilization of STC increases relative to utilization of regular UI claims.

The patterns for the lagged TUR coefficients are nearly as consistent. All 17 are negative and 13 have $t$-ratios of 2.0 or larger. In the year after the TUR increases there is a sharp falloff in STC usage. Short-time compensation usage decreases noticeably in the second year of a recessionary period. This falloff occurs even if the TUR is higher in the second year of a recession as in 2010 relative to 2009. For 16 of 17 states the percentage was higher in 2009 than in 2010. Finally, the underlying data also illustrate the severe nature of the recent recession. The highest usage of STC over the full period occurred in 2009 for 14 of 17 states.

**Table 6B.1 Regressions Explaining STC Equivalent Weeks as a Percentage of Regular Weeks, 1989–2010**

| State | Constant | TUR | TUR Lag | Trend | Adj. R² | Std. error | DW | Mean (%) | Maximum (%) |
|---|---|---|---|---|---|---|---|---|---|
| Arizona | 0.289 (2.3) | 0.064 (2.6) | −0.051 (1.7) | −0.0062 (1.4) | 0.161 | 0.121 | 2.62 | 0.297 | 0.629 |
| Arkansas | −0.149 (1.3) | 0.102 (3.6) | −0.072 (2.3) | 0.0020 (0.6) | 0.441 | 0.074 | 1.33 | 0.048 | 0.407 |
| California | −0.185 (2.3) | 0.162 (10.8) | −0.085 (4.8) | 0.0021 (0.7) | 0.890 | 0.083 | 1.82 | 0.414 | 1.053 |
| Connecticut 1992 | −0.172 (0.6) | 0.232 (3.3) | −0.170 (2.1) | 0.0106 (0.8) | 0.495 | 0.258 | 2.04 | 0.308 | 1.622 |
| Florida | 0.036 (1.1) | 0.031 (4.8) | −0.020 (2.5) | −0.0027 (2.2) | 0.584 | 0.033 | 1.50 | 0.073 | 0.183 |
| Iowa 1991 | −0.397 (1.8) | 0.339 (3.5) | −0.224 (2.1) | 0.0023 (0.3) | 0.523 | 0.168 | 2.15 | 0.110 | 1.006 |
| Kansas | 0.648 (0.8) | 0.501 (2.4) | −0.610 (2.7) | 0.0459 (2.0) | 0.377 | 0.598 | 1.86 | 0.723 | 3.237 |
| Maryland | −0.116 (3.2) | 0.063 (7.6) | −0.026 (2.6) | −0.0019 (1.9) | 0.783 | 0.030 | 1.96 | 0.048 | 0.213 |
| Massachusetts | −0.209 (2.6) | 0.107 (6.0) | −0.076 (4.1) | 0.0132 (4.2) | 0.714 | 0.094 | 1.96 | 0.132 | 0.765 |
| Minnesota 1992 | −0.216 (2.4) | 0.175 (5.3) | −0.120 (3.6) | 0.0094 (1.9) | 0.770 | 0.098 | 1.50 | 0.166 | 0.790 |
| Missouri | 0.003 (0.0) | 0.162 (5.5) | −0.138 (4.0) | 0.0275 (6.7) | 0.858 | 0.111 | 2.01 | 0.476 | 1.354 |
| New York | −0.436 (2.6) | 0.172 (5.6) | −0.101 (3.1) | 0.0201 (4.4) | 0.698 | 0.135 | 1.84 | 0.257 | 1.141 |
| Oregon | −0.524 (4.6) | 0.135 (6.5) | −0.050 (2.1) | 0.0103 (2.4) | 0.803 | 0.110 | 1.31 | 0.163 | 1.010 |
| Rhode Island 1991 | −1.410 (3.0) | 0.302 (2.9) | −0.109 (0.9) | 0.1021 (5.2) | 0.773 | 0.456 | 1.67 | 1.122 | 4.173 |
| Texas | −0.581 (1.7) | 0.178 (3.1) | −0.119 (1.8) | 0.0496 (6.4) | 0.776 | 0.192 | 0.92 | 0.345 | 1.501 |
| Vermont | 0.090 (0.4) | 0.208 (3.6) | −0.227 (4.0) | 0.0462 (6.6) | 0.744 | 0.208 | 1.75 | 0.540 | 1.511 |
| Washington | −1.128 (4.9) | 0.227 (5.7) | −0.053 (1.1) | 0.0259 (3.9) | 0.781 | 0.188 | 0.64 | 0.256 | 1.562 |

SOURCE: Regressions based on data from U.S. Department of Labor, Bureau of Labor Statistics, and OUI. Absolute values of t-ratios adjacent to coefficients.

# References

Berkeley Planning Associates. 1997. "Evaluation of Short-Time Compensation Programs: Final Report." Unemployment Insurance Occasional Paper no. 97-3. Washington, DC: U.S. Department of Labor, Employment and Training Administration.

Boeri, Tito, and Herbert Bruecker. 2011. *Short-Time Work Benefits Revisited: Some Lessons from the Great Recession*. Prepared for the Economic Policy Panel, Budapest, April 15–16.

Burda, Michael, and Jennifer Hunt. June 2011. "What Explains the German Labor Market Miracle in the Great Recession?" NBER Working Paper No. 17187. Cambridge, MA: National Bureau of Economic Research.

Crimmann, Andreas, Frank Wießner, and Lutz Bellmann. 2010. "The German Work Sharing Scheme: An Instrument for the Crisis." ILO, Conditions of Work and Employment Series no. 25. Geneva: ILO.

Hijzen, Alexander, and Danielle Venn. 2011. "The Role of Short-Time Work Schemes during the 2008–09 Recession." OECD Social, Employment and Migration Working Paper No. 115. Paris: OECD. http://dx.doi.org/10.1787/5kgkd0bbwvxp-en (accessed August 9, 2011).

Organisation for Economic Co-operation and Development (OECD). 2010. "Moving Beyond the Jobs Crisis." *Employment Outlook 2010*. Paris: OECD.

U.S. Department of Labor. Employment and Training Administration, Office of Unemployment Insurance. 2010. "Comparison of State Unemployment Insurance Laws 2010, Table 4.6." Washington, DC: U.S. Department of Labor.

Vroman, Wayne. 1992. *Short-Time Compensation in the U.S., Germany and Belgium*. Washington, DC: Urban Institute.

# 7

# Labor Market Measures in the Crisis and the Convergence of Social Models

Michele Tiraboschi
Silvia Spattini
*Adapt and Marco Biagi Centre for International and
Comparative Studies, University of Modena and Reggio Emilia*

## FRAMING THE ISSUE

Following the GDP decreases resulting from the severe economic crisis, EU member states experienced, each to a different extent, higher levels of unemployment. However, the implementation of so-called anticrisis measures limited such increases in unemployment—in some cases they were not as high as expected—in the majority of EU member states. Intending to minimize the impact of the downturn in social terms and support both companies and employees, the EU took a number of actions to drive the economic recovery and coordinate EU member states' public interventions, with member states either adapting existing labor market policies or introducing new ones (European Commission 2008).[1] In this context, the majority of member states launched ad hoc and comprehensive "anticrisis packages" consisting of a variety of measures to cope with the recession and resulting in a wide range of public policy tools aimed at reducing the impact of the crisis on the labor market.

During the economic downturn, some countries have performed much better than others. We set out to determine whether this happened by chance or if it was a consequence of the national social model and the choices governments made in applying specific labor market measures. In fact, the purpose of our study is to identify whether there were particular legal devices and policies that helped some EU member states to face and withstand the crisis better than others. Studying the different measures implemented by the member states and considering the national legal framework and labor regulations, this chapter offers some possible interpretations of the different national reactions to the crisis. These interpretations take into account EU member states' different labor market policy combinations and their social protection systems and employment protection legislation, which is also viewed as a combination of flexibility and security tools. The study has an interdisciplinary approach, though it is not an economic analysis. However, it aims to give suggestions and make some hypotheses on the effectiveness of labor market policy combinations and social models (including the relevant legal framework) in tackling the crisis, which economists may then prove through their analyses.

## THE CRISIS IN FIGURES

The starting point of the study is the set of figures describing the changes in the European labor market from the beginning of the crisis (see Figures 7.1–7.3 and Table 7.1). Between the second quarter of 2008 and the second quarter of 2009, the real GDP in the EU (27 member states) fell by almost 5 percent.

The fall in GDP caused a reduction of labor demand and, accordingly, an increase in unemployment and a decrease in employment. But, if you compare the two series of data—GDP and employment change from the previous period (Table 7.1)—the degree of the reduction is different, and in particular job losses are limited by comparison with the decrease of real GDP. As is well-known, in fact, GDP growth and employment generally evolve differently (Bell and Blanchflower 2011), since employment reacts to economic developments with a certain time lag (Hijman 2009; Mandl and Salvatore 2009).

The figures show a considerable difference in the impact of the crisis on the 27 EU member states, particularly if we compare unemployment rates in July 2008—that is, before the crisis—and July 2010. Although Spain and Ireland were regarded as emerging economies before the downturn, they reported significant increases in unemployment. More

**Figure 7.1  GDP Percentage Change from Previous Period**

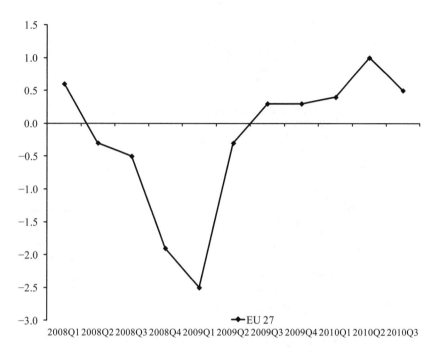

SOURCE: Eurostat, seasonally adjusted and adjusted data by working days.

specifically, the levels of unemployment almost doubled in a two-year span, an issue that has become a matter of serious concern. The same happened in the Baltic states (Estonia, Lithuania, and Latvia), which experienced the highest rates of unemployment in Europe (Figure 7.2).

Looking at the trends in Figure 7.3, Latvia, Estonia, Lithuania, Ireland, and Spain also had the highest decrease in employment rates. A case in point of the negative impact of the economic crisis on employment was Denmark. Before the crisis, Denmark had a low level of unemployment and has experienced a worsening of its labor market situation during the economic downturn. Despite Danish unemployment levels (7.3 percent in July 2010) remaining lower than the EU average (9.7 percent), Denmark experienced a critical increase in unemployment, which doubled over a two-year period. At the same time, the employment rate dropped by 4.2 percent, which was more than the EU average.

**Figure 7.2  Unemployment Rate Change and Unemployment Rate, 2010Q2**

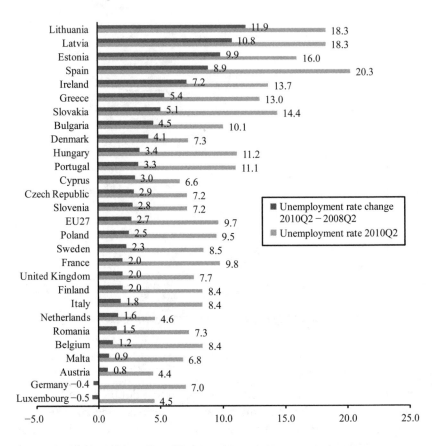

SOURCE: Authors' elaboration of Eurostat data.

The labor market is less worrisome in countries like Germany, Austria, Belgium, the Netherlands, and Italy, where the rise in the unemployment rate was in no case higher than 1.8 percent and the decrease in the rate of employment was not as significant as in the countries mentioned above. Indeed, Germany represents a unique case: after a very limited increase in unemployment (0.4 percent in July 2009 compared to July 2008), an unexpected reduction was reported in 2010, with the levels of employment experiencing a growth (ILO 2011a). Such vari-

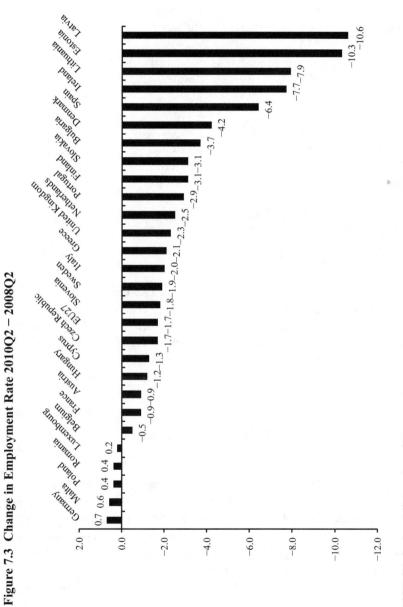

**Figure 7.3 Change in Employment Rate 2010Q2 – 2008Q2**

SOURCE: Authors' elaboration of Eurostat data.

**Table 7.1 GDP and Employment Change between 2008Q2 and 2009Q2**

| Member state | GDP | Employment | Member state | GDP | Employment |
|---|---|---|---|---|---|
| EU27 | −5.1 | −1.9 | Lithuania | −16.0 | −6.0 |
| Belgium | −4.1 | −0.2 | Luxembourg | −7.8 | 1.2 |
| Bulgaria | −4.6 | −1.8 | Hungary | −7.4 | −2.3 |
| Czech Republic | −4.8 | −0.9 | Malta | −4.4 | −0.1[a] |
| Denmark | −7.3 | −2.2 | Netherlands | −5.1 | −1.2 |
| Germany | −5.5 | −0.0 | Austria | −5.4 | −1.0 |
| Estonia | −16.5 | −9.9 | Poland | +1.4 | +0.8 |
| Ireland | −7.7 | −8.3 | Portugal | −3.0 | −2.7 |
| Greece | −2.0 | −0.7 | Romania | −8.3 | −2.0[a] |
| Spain | −4.4 | −7.0 | Slovenia | −9.5 | −1.4 |
| France | −3.1 | −1.3 | Slovakia | −4.9 | −1.5 |
| Italy | −6.4 | −1.4 | Finland | −10.2 | −2.9 |
| Cyprus | −1.7 | −0.4[a] | Sweden | −6.3 | −2.2[a] |
| Latvia | −17.3 | −13.2 | United Kingdom | −5.9 | −2.1 |

[a]Not seasonally adjusted data.
SOURCE: Eurostat, National Accounts.

ability among European countries, and the fact that the recession had little impact on some of them, seems not to be coincidental. There is some empirical evidence that the different performance levels within national labor markets could result from the diversified legal framework of labor regulation and existing labor market policies and institutions, along with new measures taken by governments to combat the crisis.

## ANTICRISIS MEASURES ACROSS EUROPE

The combination of several factors at the national level produced, in fact, 27 different ways in which the economic downturn hit the EU member states. In addition, there were 27 different responses to the crisis. Each country has adopted a set of measures—not a single action—among which it is possible to identify the most frequently implemented ones (European Commission 2009). Moreover, it is necessary to take into consideration that labor market policies adopted by national governments vary considerably, especially in terms of issues concerning the role played by social partners in each country. Each country's participation in the development and implementation of anticrisis measures and with the adjustment of existing labor market tools differs across Europe. Differences are also found when one considers the level and the extent of the involvement of each EU member state in public policy design. Policy development and implementation depend on the diversity of functions performed by the social dialogue at the time, and the power of each government.

In Austria, Belgium, Italy, Germany, and the Netherlands—countries with a well-established social partnership—agreements between social partners contributed considerably to the creation of stimulus packages. With regard to collective bargaining, opening clauses allowed company-level agreements to deviate from sectoral collective agreements in order to cut costs and safeguard employment (i.e., deviation from the general framework). These agreements usually envisage an extension in working time without full compensation in pay, cuts in working time, cuts in benefits, or delays in agreed pay increases (ILO 2011b).

In order to assess the effectiveness of the adopted policies, it is necessary to review existing legislation and classify measures implemented by every European country in accordance with a simple scheme. The classification of policy measures is a preliminary step for verifying whether there is a relationship between patterns of labor market policies adopted by member states and the trends of the national labor market during the crisis. To date, key reports from the European Commission (Arpaia et al. 2010; Hurley et al. 2009; Mandl and Salvatore 2009), the OECD (2010), and EU institutions (Employment Committee [EMCO] and the European Commission [EC] 2010) have analyzed public interventions in the labor market. In particular, the Eurofound has provided a useful classification of crisis-related measures implemented in the EU member states (see Table 7.2) (Hurley et al. 2009; Mandl and Salvatore 2009). This classification is based on three different types of interventions: 1) measures to create employment or to promote reintegration, 2) measures to maintain employment, and 3) income support measures for the unemployed.

**Table 7.2  Classification of Labor Market Measures**

| Measures to create employment or to promote reintegration | Income support measures for the unemployed | Measures to maintain employment |
|---|---|---|
| Job matching, counseling, career guidance:<br>• Improving public employment services<br>• Support for workers to find a job<br><br>Incentives for companies to employ additional workers<br>• Wage subsidies<br>• Reduction of/exemption from non-wage labor costs<br>• Nonfinancial incentives<br><br>(Re-) Training of the unemployed:<br>• Income support while in training<br>• Advice/consultancy, skill assessment tools<br>• Provision/organization of training<br>• Contribution to training costs<br><br>Mobility grants<br>• Tax incentives<br>• Travel/accommodation allowances<br>• Repatriation allowances | Unemployment benefits<br>• Eligibility criteria<br>• Amount<br>• Duration of support for entitlement groups of workers<br><br>Other instruments<br>• early retirement payment<br>• child benefits<br>• housing/heating | Support of short-time work or temporary layoff<br>• Wage subsidies<br>• Social security contributions<br><br>Training support<br>• Advice/consultancy to enterprises<br>• Contribution to training costs<br>• Wage subsidy<br><br>Reduction/deferral of nonwage labor costs<br>• Social security contributions<br>• Taxes<br><br>Direct enterprise support<br>• risk-capital schemes, guarantees, direct subsidies<br>• reduction of company taxes |

Support of self-employment
- Advice/consultancy, training
- Start-up grants
- Reduction/deferral of social security payments

Indirect enterprise support
- Public investment
- Incentives for consumers' purchases

## Measures to Create Employment and to Promote Reintegration

Measures to create employment (Mandl and Salvatore 2009) aim to promote the hiring of employees by means of economic incentives, mainly consisting of a reduction of nonwage labor costs and wage subsidies or public sector job creation. In some countries (Germany, France, Italy, Portugal, Slovenia, and Sweden), the economic incentives for companies are provided for hiring special target groups. Support measures for self-employment, based on the provision of consultancy and training (the U.K. and Bulgaria), or the reduction/deferment of social security payments also falls within this category. Several member states (Austria, Lithuania, Italy, Portugal, and the U.K.) have introduced or extended subsidies for business start-ups.

Measures to promote reintegration into employment (Hurley et al. 2009), put into action by employment services, try to enhance the transition from unemployment to employment by addressing job mismatch, supporting job matching by means of counseling, career guidance, search assistance, activation measures, and by increasing employability through training. Efforts have been made to improve and adapt public employment services in order to manage the higher number of "clients" (for example, hiring additional staff, as in Germany, Norway, Spain, and the U.K.) and to economically support private employment agencies through economic and/or normative incentives (the Netherlands and Italy). In the same vein, and with the goal of making workers more willing to accept a new job, mobility grants are envisaged (Slovakia, Lithuania, and the Czech Republic). In Belgium, for instance, employees who agree to relocate in order to accept a job offer obtain tax benefits.

## Income Support for Unemployed People

Income support for unemployed people (Hurley et al. 2009; Mandl and Salvatore 2009) mainly consists of unemployment benefits, provided to reduce the socioeconomic consequences of job loss. Unemployment benefit systems exist in every EU member state, even though amendments (in some cases temporary) have been made at a national level to their regulations in order to respond to the increased number of unemployed people resulting from the crisis. Relevant changes have been particularly concerned with the following areas: eligibility criteria, amount, duration of entitlement, and beneficiaries. More specifically, some countries relaxed the rules for entitlement to unemployment benefits (France, Finland, and Sweden), while others extended the duration: Romania has envisaged an extension of 3 months, Latvia extended the unemployment benefit receipt period to 9 months, and in Poland it moved from 12 to 18 months. In the Czech Republic, the government has opted for an increase in the amount of funds, while Italy introduced (on a temporary basis) special benefits for quasi-subordinate workers.

## Measures to Maintain Employment

Measures to maintain employment are intended to prevent dismissals and preserve existing jobs. Among these instruments, the main ones are short-time work (STW) arrangements and compensation.

### Short-time work schemes

Short-time work may take the form of a temporary reduction in working time or a temporary layoff. In both cases, the employment relationship between employer and employee persists and the arrangements have a limited duration (Arpaia et al. 2010). In the case of STW, compensation for income loss is usually envisaged in the form of social security payments. This compensation is either publicly funded—by means of taxes—or based on social security contributions. Nevertheless, STW compensation systems across Europe differ considerably from each other in terms of procedures, degree of involvement of trade unions, "back-to-normal" plans, coverage, compensations amount, and eligibility criteria. Moreover, it is possible to distinguish between well-established systems and new schemes introduced to face the crisis (Table 7.3).

In the first case (which includes Germany, Austria, Belgium, France, and Italy, among others), the compensation system is part of the unemployment benefit (insurance) system, in that employers and employees pay social contributions to a fund or to the UI system so that in the event of STW or temporary layoff, employees are covered by this fund for the lost income as a consequence of a working hours reduction. Conversely, in member states (such as the Netherlands, Poland, Hungary, and Slovakia) that introduced, whether temporary or not, STW compensations as

**Table 7.3  Different Systems of Short-Time Work**

| Group I—Existing and/or adapted systems (Germany, Austria, Belgium, France, Italy, etc.) | Group II—Systems introduced to face the crisis (the Netherlands, Poland, Hungary, Slovakia, etc.) |
| --- | --- |
| STW arrangements are part of the unemployment benefit/insurance system | STW arrangements are not part of the unemployment benefit/insurance system |
| The employer and (in some cases) the employees pay social contributions to a fund or to the UI system | STW arrangements are funded by taxes |
| In the event of STW or temporary layoff, employees are covered for the lost income | |

a new measure during the crisis, such new arrangements are not part of the UI system and therefore they are funded by the state through taxes.

STW compensation systems may also be classified on the basis of their function (Arpaia et al. 2010). In some national systems, they are part-time unemployment benefits. This means that employees working reduced hours or on temporary layoff are regarded as people working on a part-time basis seeking full-time employment. In some cases, they may have to be available for a new job despite the fact that the employment contract with their current employer is still in force. Regardless of function, in the majority of EU member states, this is true even if STW schemes envisage lost income compensation within the unemployment insurance system. Indeed, STW schemes represent a form of job protection against dismissal.

With reference to this measure, it is possible to point out that it might be beneficial to different actors involved in the national economic arena. Needless to say, employees benefit from STW schemes since measures of this kind avoid dismissal and help maintain existing jobs, at the same time ensuring income support by compensating lost income. However, STW schemes also have many advantages for employers. First, these arrangements allow companies to preserve human capital and skills that will be necessary in the recovery phase. Second, they reduce potential costs related to personnel turnover, dismissal, the recruitment process, and training. Governments view STW compensation systems as convenient measures, as they help maintain social peace and cohesion in that employers and employees share the impact of a downturn. Finally, such arrangements represent a flexible tool for governments, such that they are able to control, to some extent, the adjustment of the labor market.

## THE EFFECTIVENESS OF LABOR MARKET MEASURES

This research tries to identify the system and policies that provide a higher level of effectiveness in tackling the crisis and unemployment, and to collect information that could be useful on a general basis while deciding which labor market policies to implement and which legal framework to apply. It is generally acknowledged that it takes time to evaluate the effectiveness of labor market measures. However, in a joint paper, EMCO and the EC provide some evidence for the effectiveness of the main labor market policies adopted and implemented by EU member states during the crisis, and, more generally, they review evaluations of the effectiveness of similar measures implemented in the past (EMCO and EC 2010). The OECD, on the other hand, gives evidence for the effectiveness of STW schemes applied during this recession (OECD 2010).

Considering the three different types of labor market policies examined in this chapter (measures to create employment or to promote reintegration, measures to maintain employment, and income support for unemployed), measures to maintain employment in the form of STW arrangements, wage subsidies, or nonwage cost reductions are deemed to have been most successful in limiting the decrease in employment rates (Governatori et al. 2010) and the rise of unemployment, by preventing layoffs. Among measures of this kind implemented by the member states, some of them—particularly STW schemes—have proved more effective than others in preserving jobs (EMCO and EC 2010; OECD 2010). Nevertheless, researchers point out critical issues related to STW arrangements, such as the fact that they may artificially maintain employment in declining industries instead of allowing for an efficient reallocation of employment. There is general agreement about the potential negative impact—the deadweight loss—from distortions due to this policy (OECD 2010). However, countermeasures can be taken to address these distortions. In particular, STW schemes can be provided for a shorter period of time and can be arranged on the basis of more precise eligibility criteria.

Regarding measures to create employment, job subsidies consisting of hiring incentives or the reduction of nonwage labor costs are effective in terms of job creation, but they are costly measures that can lead to negative consequences in terms of the deadweight effect. At the same time, public sector job creation is less likely than other policies to provide positive impacts (Kluve 2006, 2008).

With respect to measures that promote reintegration, training has a modest positive impact on employment. This kind of impact is more likely to be associated with times of high unemployment. But, in general, positive training effects become evident in the long run, and it is not clear whether there is a positive or negative relation between the economic cycle and the effectiveness of this kind of measure. Therefore, it is difficult to state how effective training programs may be during the economic crisis (Kluve 2008). On the other hand, job search assistance and activation measures have a positive impact on employment and are effective in the short run, but they need an economic context characterized by a growing or stable labor demand. In fact, only if there is labor demand is it possible to support job search and matching and help with reintegration into the labor market. For this reason, such measures are mainly appropriate in the recovery phase.

Generally speaking, income supports for the unemployed may have a negative effect on unemployment (OECD 2006) since their generosity (replacement rate and duration) discourage job search and reintegration into the labor market. In order to reduce the negative effects in terms of efficiency, some adjustments can be and have been made, such as decreasing the amount of benefits and reducing the period through which such support is provided. In addition, unemployment benefits have to be made conditional on availability for suitable work and participation in active labor market policies (ALMPs) and activation policies (OECD 2010). The majority of EU member states have moved in this direction, since in their systems, as shown in Table 7.4, unemployment benefit recipients are required to actively search for work (in 18 cases out of 27), to be immediately available for suitable work (almost all member states) and accept suitable job offers, and to be ready to

**Table 7.4  Obligations of Unemployment Benefit Recipients**

| Country | Active job search | Participation in ALMP | Available for suitable work |
|---|---|---|---|
| Belgium | x | | x |
| Bulgaria | | x | |
| Czech Republic | | | |
| Denmark | x | x | x |
| Germany | x | x | x |
| Estonia | x | | x |
| Greece | | x | x |
| Spain | x | x | x |
| France | x | x | |
| Ireland | x | | x |
| Italy | | x | x |
| Cyprus | | x | x |
| Latvia | x | | x |
| Lithuania | x | x | x |
| Luxembourg | | x | x |
| Hungary | x | x | x |
| Malta | | | x |
| The Netherlands | x | | x |
| Austria | | x | x |
| Poland | | | x |
| Portugal | x | | x |
| Romania | x | | x |
| Finland | x | x | x |
| Slovenia | x | x | |
| Slovakia | x | x | x |
| Sweden | x | x | x |
| United Kingdom | x | x | x |

participate in the ALMPs (in 17 cases out of 27) commonly agreed on in an individual action plan or client contract. The plan or contract is established between the unemployment benefit recipient and the public employment service and identifies the rights and duties of both parties. Moreover, in the view of assuring the effectiveness of this conditionality, sanctions are applied to recipients in cases of noncompliance with the above-mentioned obligations.

## THE ROLE OF EMPLOYMENT SERVICES IN THE
## IMPLEMENTATION OF ALMPs

Public employment services are generally able to implement labor market measures. Therefore, they play a key role in supporting the (re)integration of the unemployed into the labor market and, in the end, employment levels. It is well known that the effective implementation of labor market policies depends on the efficiency of public employment services (EC 2002). However, they may achieve their goals not only by acting directly through their organizations, but also through cooperation with other actors and stakeholders (i.e., other public organizations, social security institutions, social partners, other service providers, or education and training providers). From this perspective, European institutions themselves encourage the collaboration of public employment services with other service providers (Council of the European Union 2001, 2002; EC 1998). This relationship may even take the form of subcontracting services to private employment agencies, which generally allows public employment services to better deliver specific services for particular target groups among the unemployed (Anderson et al. 2009).

Employment services also play an important role with regard to the effectiveness of the conditionality of unemployment benefits on participation in ALMPs and on accepting suitable job offers. Looking at public employment services, the purpose of a consistent strategy is to facilitate the return of the unemployed and unemployment benefit recipients into the labor market. To achieve this, public employment services and social security institutions must cooperate closely, which may develop into a merger between the two (Anderson et al. 2009). Indeed, in a number of EU member states (see Table 7.5) there is a single institution responsible for the provision of employment services and unemployment benefits. This trend is confirmed by recent mergers in France and the Netherlands in 2009.

**Table 7.5  Institutions Responsible for the Provision of Employment Services and Unemployment Benefits**

| | |
|---|---|
| Austria | Arbeitsmarktservice (AMS) |
| France | Pôle emploi: (ANPE + Assedic) |
| Germany | Bundesagentur für Arbeit (Federal Employment Agency) |
| Estonia | Eesti Töötukassa |
| Greece | Greek Manpower Employment Organization (OAED) |
| Luxembourg | Administration de l'emploi (ADEM) |
| Slovenia | Employment Service of Slovenia |
| The Netherlands | Location for Work and Income: Centre for Work and Income + Uitvoeringsinstitut werknemersverzekeringen (Employee Insurance Agency) |
| United Kingdom | Jobcentre Plus (merger of Employment Service and Benefits Agency, 2002) |

## PUBLIC EXPENDITURE ON LABOR MARKET POLICIES

The question of effectiveness of labor market policies is fundamental not only with regard to crisis-related measures, but also for EU member states because of a rise in budgetary constraints. European institutions have reported that in 2009 EU countries increased their expenditure on labor market interventions and income supports by 0.7 percent of annual GDP, while before the crisis, public expenditure on labor market policies had experienced a decline (EMCO and EC 2010). In fact, in 2008, public expenditure on labor market policies in the EU amounted to just 1.6 percent of total EU-27 GDP, although there was considerable variation between member states (see Figure 7.4).[2] For this reason, EU governments need to be aware of the most effective policy mix in order to direct the public expenditure. It is interesting to compare data on labor market policy expenditures and trends in unemployment rates among the different EU countries during the crisis. The data on public expenditures for all countries are available only 18–20 months after the reference period, and as a result, Eurostat provides, at the moment, only data for 2008.

154

Figure 7.4 Total LMP Expenditure and Unemployment Rate Change 2009Q2–2008Q2

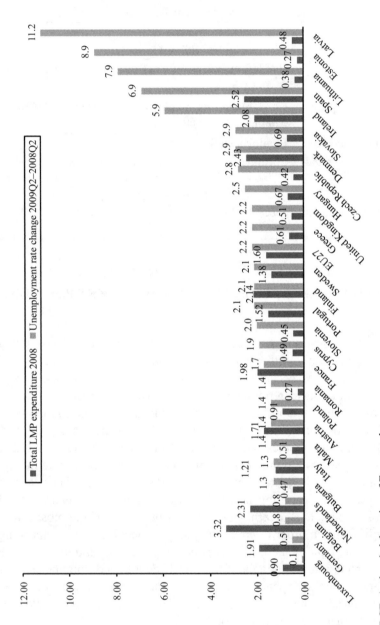

SOURCE: Authors' elaboration of Eurostat data.

In any case, considering that the impact of labor market policies (LMPs) on the labor market requires a period of time to become evident, it seems reasonable to compare data on public expenditure for 2008 and unemployment rate growth over the last two years. Member states that had the lowest increases in unemployment rates in 2009 compared to 2008 were those that spent the most on labor market policies in 2008. As Figure 7.4 shows, Belgium, Germany, the Netherlands, and Austria spent more than 1.8 percent of their GDP on LMPs and saw very small levels of unemployment growth or even declines in unemployment during this period. Figure 7.5 shows that this trend is confirmed even if we compare the growth in unemployment rate between 2008 and 2010 and the labor market policies expenditure for 2008.

When the data on public expenditures for 2009 are available for all countries, it will also be interesting to verify if and to what extent the increase in unemployment affected public expenditure.

## POLICIES ADAPTED OR ADOPTED BY THE EU MEMBER STATES

By analyzing the different measures implemented by the EU member states, it is possible to observe a relationship between different combinations of labor market measures applied by EU countries and their social models. From this perspective, it is necessary to consider *in toto* the set of labor market policies—both new and amended—that the EU member states put into action to face the crisis. Table 7.6 represents, without the pretention of being exhaustive, the measures adopted or adapted (if already existing) by each EU member state against this background. The EU countries have been identified by their levels of unemployment rate growth (considering the difference between July 2010 and July 2008), ranked from the best to the worst in terms of performance. It should be pointed out that those countries with the most significant increases in unemployment rates are those that did not envisage or did not amend existing STW schemes.

On the other hand, EU member states with good labor market performance, such as Germany, Luxembourg, Belgium, Austria, and, to some extent, Italy, already had measures of this kind in their labor mar-

156

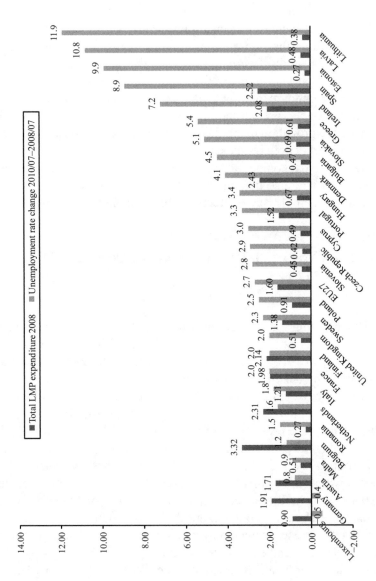

**Figure 7.5 Total LMP Expenditure and Unemployment Rate Change 2010/07–2008/07**

■ Total LMP expenditure 2008     ■ Unemployment rate change 2010/07–2008/07

SOURCE: Authors' elaboration of Eurostat data.

ket systems. Furthermore, these countries made such labor market policies more flexible over the past few years, in consideration of the needs of the moment, and improved or adapted these policies by combining them with training and/or activation measures. Other well-performing countries, such as the Netherlands and Romania, have introduced (even on a temporary basis) STW schemes to face the recession.

The next step is to contextualize these different combinations of policies in the wider regulatory framework of national labor markets. In this view, two main social models are taken into consideration: the welfare system model and the flexicurity model (Table 7.7).

The first system is characterized by rigid employment protection legislation (particularly in the event of dismissal), an ungenerous unemployment benefit system, and a minimum level of implementation of ALMPs and activation of policies through public employment services. It is noteworthy that the welfare system model developed over the years an active component, which in the past was very limited or absent. On the other hand, the flexicurity model is based on a nonrestrictive dismissal protection legislation, a generous unemployment benefit system, high levels of implementation of ALMPs and activation policies, and efficient public employment services. Examples of the first model can be found in countries like Germany, Austria, Belgium, and Italy, while Denmark has always been the model for flexicurity, together with Finland, Sweden, Norway, and the Netherlands.

## THE EFFECTIVENESS OF SOCIAL MODELS

By looking at the labor market performance of the EU member states, and by considering their social models, some interesting remarks and comments are possible.

Regarding growth in the unemployment rate during the crisis, Germany, Belgium, Austria, and to some extent Italy, are considered to be the countries with the lowest increases. The social model of all these EU member states is classified as a welfare system. On the other hand, Denmark, which, as mentioned, is regarded as a role model of flexicurity, experienced a high increase in unemployment. This country has been and still is, in fact, an interesting case with reference to the per-

**Table 7.6  Policies Mix**

| | Change in unemployment rate 2010Q2– 2008Q2 | STW compensations | Training activities during the time off/training support for employees | Reduction/ deferral of nonwage labor costs | Public expenditure |
|---|---|---|---|---|---|
| Luxembourg | −0.5 | + | + | | |
| Germany | −0.4 | + | + | + | |
| Austria | 0.8 | + | + | | |
| Malta | 0.9 | | + | | |
| Belgium | 1.2 | + | + | + | |
| Romania | 1.5 | new | | + | |
| Netherlands | 1.6 | new | compulsory | + | |
| Italy | 1.8 | + | + | | |
| Finland | 2.0 | | | | |
| United Kingdom | 2.0 | | + | | |
| France | 2.0 | + | + | | + |
| Sweden | 2.3 | | | + | |
| Poland | 2.5 | new | | | |
| EU 27 | 2.7 | | | | |
| Slovenia | 2.8 | new | compulsory | | |
| Czech Republic | 2.9 | new | compulsory | + | |
| Cyprus | 3.0 | | + | | |
| Portugal | 3.3 | + | + | + | |
| Hungary | 3.4 | new | compulsory | + | |
| Denmark | 4.1 | | | | |
| Bulgaria | 4.5 | new | | + | |
| Slovakia | 5.1 | | | + | |
| Greece | 5.4 | | + | | |
| Ireland | 7.2 | | + | | |
| Spain | 8.9 | | | | + |
| Estonia | 9.9 | | | | |
| Latvia | 10.8 | | + | | |
| Lithuania | 11.9 | | + | | |

| Income tax cut | Incentives to employ additional workers | Direct enterprise support (loan guarantees, low-interest loans) | Mobility grants | (Re-)training of unemployed people | Improving employment services | Unemployment benefits (amendments) |
|---|---|---|---|---|---|---|
|  |  |  |  | + |  |  |
|  | + | + |  |  | + |  |
|  |  |  |  | + |  |  |
|  |  |  | + |  |  |  |
|  |  | + |  |  | + | + |
|  | + | + |  | + | + |  |
|  |  |  |  | + |  |  |
|  |  |  |  | + | + | + |
|  | + |  |  |  | + | + |
|  | + | + |  | + |  | + |
|  | + |  |  |  | + | + |
| + |  | + |  | + |  | + |
|  | + | + |  |  |  |  |
|  |  |  | + |  |  | + |
|  | + |  |  |  |  |  |
|  | + | + |  |  |  |  |
|  |  |  |  |  |  | + |
|  | + |  |  |  | + |  |
|  |  |  | + |  |  |  |
|  | + |  |  |  |  |  |
|  |  |  |  | + |  | + |
|  |  |  |  | + | + |  |
| + |  | + |  | + |  | + |
| + |  | + |  | + |  | + |
| + |  | + | + |  |  |  |

**Table 7.7 Welfare and Flexicurity Systems Comparison**

| Systems | Employment protection legislation | Unemployment benefit system | STW and layoff compensations | Active labor market policies (ALMPs) public employment services (PES) |
|---|---|---|---|---|
| Welfare systems (Central and Southern Europe) | Stringent dismissal protection legislation (individual and collective) | Nongenerous: Short duration Low replacement rate | Yes | Low level of activities and implementation of few ALMPs |
| Flexicurity systems (Northern Europe) | Nonrestrictive dismissal protection legislation | Generous: Long duration High replacement rate | No or very limited as partial unemployment benefit | High level of activities and implementation of many ALMPs |

formance of the labor market during the crisis. Before the crisis, this system ensured a low unemployment rate and a quick reintegration of jobseekers into the labor market. During the crisis, however, this system proved to have some shortcomings. In fact, by September 2009, Denmark had doubled its level of unemployment: from 3.2 percent in July 2008 to 6.5 percent in September 2009 (Denmark reached its highest level of unemployment, 7.4 percent, in April 2010).

The aim of this system is not to prevent dismissal but rather to support a quick job-to-job transition and reintegration into the labor market. Nevertheless, if the labor demand is low, then reintegration is impossible or very difficult. In addition, Denmark does not envisage a "real" STW compensation system even though companies may use STW arrangements and employees involved are eligible for part-time unemployment benefits. Employees must fulfill the contributory requirements for eligibility for total unemployment benefits and have to be available for a new working activity despite the fact that the employment contract with their current employer is still in force. However, in practice this provision is not strictly applied if the employee has the possibility of staying with his or her current company.

Finland, Sweden, and the Netherlands (plus Norway, which is not an EU member) also use the flexicurity system. While they had better labor market performance than Denmark during the recession, these countries still experienced an increase in their unemployment rates amounting to more than 2 percent (the Netherlands was the only exception, with an increase of 1.6 percent). There is an important difference between Denmark and the other flexicurity countries—employment protection legislation. Denmark has liberally oriented employment protection legislation, while the other flexicurity countries, which utilize a welfare system, have more stringent employment protection legislation (see Table 7.8). Among flexicurity countries, the Netherlands is the only country characterized by a lower rise in its unemployment rate. It introduced a temporary STW compensation, while Finland's is similar to Denmark, and Sweden does not envisage any.

On the basis of these observations, it clearly emerges that countries utilizing the welfare system model had lower increases in unemployment rates, while flexicurity countries, especially Denmark, experienced higher rises. Thus, the welfare system model appears to be more effective in facing the crisis, while the flexicurity system has difficul-

**Table 7.8  OECD Employment Protection Legislation Index**

| Countries | OECD EPL index |
|---|---|
| Germany | 2.63 |
| Luxembourg | 3.39 |
| Malta | — |
| Austria | 2.41 |
| Romania | — |
| Belgium | 2.61 |
| **Netherlands** | **2.23** |
| Italy | 2.58 |
| **Finland** | **2.29** |
| United Kingdom | 1.09 |
| France | 3.00 |
| **Sweden** | **2.06** |
| Poland | 2.41 |
| European Union | 2.41 |
| Czech Republic | 2.32 |
| Portugal | 2.84 |
| Slovenia | 2.76 |
| Hungary | 2.11 |
| Cyprus | — |
| **Denmark** | **1.91** |
| Bulgaria | — |
| Greece | 2.97 |
| Slovakia | 2.13 |
| Ireland | 1.39 |
| Spain | 3.11 |
| Lithuania | — |
| Latvia | — |
| Estonia | 2.39 |

ties controlling the increase in unemployment. This situation seems to depend on the presence in welfare system models of two complementary and interrelated elements: STW arrangements and a stringent regulation against (individual or collective) dismissal. However, considering social models and labor market policy combinations applied by EU member states, there is no unique "best solution" to tackle "different kinds" of economic recessions. It is also important to understand the context and the legal framework in which any possible solution has to be implemented.

## CONCLUSION: LESSON FROM THE CRISIS

The financial crisis has created a sort of laboratory in which it was possible to conduct natural experiments on the functioning of different national systems, created through a combination of the social security system, employment protection legislation, the public employment services system, and labor market policies. Over the last two decades, when considering labor market policies to be implemented by European countries, the OECD and European Commission put an emphasis mainly on *active* labor market policies rather than passive ones, thus supporting mainly public interventions utilizing active measures. Therefore, before the crisis, these international institutions largely recommended flexicurity principles dominated by external flexibility and employment security based on nonrestrictive or low-restrictive employment protection legislation (and dismissal protection legislation), supported by a generous unemployment benefit system, efficient public employment services, and high levels of ALMPs. From this point of view, prevailing measures aimed to create employment or, better yet, promote reintegration, giving momentum to job-to-job transition. In fact, by launching the EU flexicurity strategy, the EU promoted internal and external flexicurity "accompanied by secure transition from job to job" (European Commission 2007).

Looking from this standpoint at policy packages applied by EU member states, at the beginning of the crisis there was a critical view of STW arrangements. In fact, observers and commentators constantly pointed out the labor market distortions and limitations associated with these schemes. One frequent criticism was that since they were income support measures, they demonstrated the passive nature of labor market policy. But more recently, and perhaps thanks to the effectiveness in tackling the crisis, authors look at these schemes in a different way. Indeed, a report from the Eurofound (Mandl et al. 2010) describing the effectiveness of STW schemes tries to link these measures to the flexicurity principle by stressing how they serve the implementation of flexicurity. Considering how STW schemes function, it is easy to see them as tools for flexicurity, combining internal flexibility and job and income security. In fact, the possibility of reducing work hours (up to zero hours) allows internal flexibility for employers (based exactly on flexible working-time arrangements). At the same time, this provision prevents dismissals and helps employees stay in their current positions, enhancing job security. Moreover, wage compensation linked to STW arrangements ensures income security for the employees, thanks to the continuity of income granted through either a wage or unemployment benefits.

Considering now the other types of labor market policy measures mentioned above in terms of flexicurity, measures to promote reintegration and to create employment are fundamental resources for guaranteeing employment security, at least through continuity of employment, although not necessarily with the same employer. On the other hand, income support for unemployed people has the obvious purpose of ensuring income security in case of dismissal and can be seen as complementary to external flexibility. Before the crisis, EU institutions pressed for welfare systems to move toward the flexicurity model. But the economic downturn raised the awareness of the fact that the EU formulation of the flexicurity strategy was suitable for a period of economic growth and to face structural unemployment, which needs particular measures to support (re-)integration by addressing job mismatch, supporting job matching by means of counseling, career guidance, search assistance, activation measures, and by increasing employability through training.

Indeed, a flexicurity strategy based on external flexibility and employment security was not able to withstand the impact of the recession. In such a situation, in fact, in order to limit the related socioeconomic consequences, policy measures to maintain employment and keep employees at work turned out to be indispensable. A lesson has been provided by the crisis: both welfare and flexicurity models underwent changes due to the adaptation or introduction of specific labor market policies to face the crisis. For example, welfare models have developed activation and training measures, while some flexicurity models adopted some kind of STW arrangements. Each model has taken up some elements of the other one, particularly those useful to tackle the crisis. This process of adjustment due to the recession resulted in a convergence of the two social models.

## Notes

1. At the international level, the International Labour Conference (2009) adopted a Global Jobs pact.
2. At the moment of closing the article, Eurostat provided data for 2009 just for a few EU member states.

## References

Andersen, Tine, Martin Eggert Hansen, Josina Moltesen, Danish Technological Institute, Lizzi Feiler, Rudolf Götz, Ton Wilthagen, Irmgard Borghouts, Alex Nunn, and Leeds Metropolitan University. 2009. *The Role of the Public Employment Services Related to "Flexicurity" in the European Labour Markets*. VC/2007/0927 Policy and Business Analysis. Copenhagen: Danish Technology Institute.

Arpaia, A., N. Curci, E. Meyermans, J. Peschner, and F. Pierini. 2010. *Short-Time Working Arrangements as Response to Cyclical Fluctuations*. European Economy Occasional Papers 64. Luxembourg: European Commission.

Bell, David N. F., and David G. Blanchflower. 2011. "The Crisis, Policy Reactions and Attitudes to Globalization and Jobs." IZA Discussion Paper No. 5680. Bonn, Germany: Institute for the Study of Labor (IZA).

Council of the European Union. 2001. "Council Decision of 19 January 2001 on Guidelines for Member States' Employment Policies for the Year 2001 (2001/63/EC)." *Official Journal of the European Communities* L22(January 24): 18–24.

———. 2002. "Council Decision of 18 February on Guidelines for Member States' Employment Policies for the Year 2002 (2002/177/EC)." *Official Journal of the European Communities* L60(March 1): 60–69.

Employment Committee (EMCO) and European Commission (EC). 2010. *The Choice of Effective Employment Policies Measures to Mitigate Jobless Recovery in Times of Fiscal Austerity*. Brussels: EMCO and EC.

European Commission (EC). 1998. *Modernising Public Employment Services to Support the European Employment Strategy*. 641 final, November 13. Brussels: Commission of the European Communities.

———. 2002. *Draft Joint Employment Report 2002*. 621 final, November 13. Brussels: Commission of the European Communities.

————. 2007. *Towards Common Principles of Flexicurity: More and Better Jobs through Flexibility and Security.* 359 final, June 27. Luxembourg: European Communities.

————. 2008. *A European Economic Recovery Plan.* 800 final, November 26. Brussels: Commission of the European Communities.

————. 2009. *Recovering from the Crisis—27 Ways of Tackling the Employment Challenge.* Luxembourg: European Communities.

Governatori, Matteo, Magdalena Grzegorzewska, João Medeiros, Eric Meyermans, Paul Minty, Jörg Peschner, Johan Van der Valk, John Hurley, and Frédéric Lagneaux. 2010. *Employment in Europe 2010.* Luxembourg: European Commission.

Hijman, Remko. 2009. "The Impact of the Crisis on Employment." *Eurostat Statistics in Focus* 79: 1–8.

Hurley, John, Irene Mandl, Donald Storrie, and Terry Ward. 2009. *Restructuring in Recession.* ERM Report 2009. Dublin: European Foundation for the Improvement of Living and Working Conditions (Eurofound).

International Labour Conference. 2009. *Recovering from the Crisis: A Global Jobs Pact.* Geneva: International Labour Office.

International Labour Organization (ILO). 2011a. *Germany: A Job-Centred Approach.* Studies on Growth with Equity. Geneva: ILO.

————. 2011b. *Making Recovery Sustainable: Lessons from Country Innovations.* Geneva: ILO.

Kluve, Jochen. 2006. "The Effectiveness of European Active Labor Market Policy." IZA Discussion Paper No. 2018. Bonn, Germany: Institute for the Study of Labor (IZA).

————. 2008. "The Capacity of Active Labour Market Policies to Combat European Unemployment." In *New European Approaches to Long-Term Unemployment*, Germana Di Domenico and Silvia Spattini, eds. Alphen aan den Rijn, the Netherlands: Kluwer Law International, pp. 27–37.

Mandl, Irene, John Hurley, Massimiliano Mascherini, Donald Storrie, Andrea Broughton, Radoslaw Owczarzak, Sara Riso, and Lidia Salvatore. 2010. *Extending Flexicurity—The Potential of Short-Time Working Schemes.* Luxembourg: European Foundation for the Improvement of Living and Working Conditions, Publications Office of the European Union.

Mandl, Irene, and Lidia Salvatore. 2009. *Tackling the Recession: Employment-Related Public Initiatives in the EU Member States and Norway.* Dublin: European Foundation for the Improvement of Living and Working Conditions (Eurofound).

Organisation for Economic Co-operation and Development (OECD). 2006. *Boosting Jobs and Incomes.* Employment Outlook 2006. Paris: OECD.

————. 2010. *Moving beyond the Jobs Crisis.* Employment Outlook 2010. Paris: OECD.

# Authors

Lauren Appelbaum is a researcher with the Institute for Research on Labor and Employment at the University of California-Los Angeles.

Vera Brusentsev is a visiting assistant professor of economics at Swarthmore College.

William Darity Jr. is a professor of public policy, African and African-American studies, and economics at Duke University. He is also the chair of the Department of African and African-American Studies and the director of the Research Network on Racial and Ethnic Inequality.

Timothy M. Diette is an assistant professor of economics at Washington and Lee University.

Richard B. Freeman is the Herbert Ascherman Professor of Economics at Harvard University and codirector of the Labor and Worklife Program at Harvard Law School. He is also Senior Research Fellow on Labour Markets at the Centre for Economic Performance, part of the London School of Economics. He directs the Science and Engineering Workforce Project at the National Bureau of Economic Research.

Arthur H. Goldsmith is the Jackson T. Stephens Professor of Economics at Washington and Lee University.

Darrick Hamilton is an associate professor of urban policy at the New School.

Hilbrand Oldenhuis is a senior researcher at the Centre of Applied Labour Market Research and Innovation, Hanze University of Applied Sciences.

Louis Polstra is a professor of labor participation at the Centre of Applied Labour Market Research and Innovation, Hanze University of Applied Sciences.

John Schmitt is a senior economist with the Center for Economic and Policy Research.

Silvia Spattini is a research fellow at Adapt and the Marco Biagi Centre for International and Comparative Studies, University of Modena and Reggio Emilia.

Michele Tiraboschi is a professor of labor law and industrial relations at the University of Modena and Reggio Emilia and director of the Marco Biagi Centre for International and Comparative Studies.

Till von Wachter is an associate professor of economics at the University of California-Los Angeles.

Wayne Vroman is a senior fellow at the Urban Institute.

# Index

The italic letters *f, n,* and *t* following a page number indicate that the subject information of the heading is within a figure, note, or table, respectively, on that page.

Active labor market policies (ALMPs), 56, 163
  Denmark and, 44–45, 45*f,* 48, 54, 59*n*10
  EU, to reintegrate unemployed into employment, 10, 151*t,* 160*t*
  income support dependent on participation in, 150–151
ALMPs. *See* Active labor market policies
Arizona, STC requirements in, 131*t,* 133–134, 135*t*
Arkansas, STC requirements in, 131*t,* 133–134, 135*t*
Asia. *See* China; Japan
Australia, 45*f,* 46*f,* 47*f*
  EPL in, 46, 48*f*
  unemployment in, 38*f,* 40, 41*f*
Austria, 45*f,* 46*f,* 48*f,* 146
  employment in, 140, 141*f,* 142*t,* 153*t*
  LMPs of, 154*t,* 155, 156*t,* 157, 158*t*–159*t*
  STW in, 52*f,* 147, 148*t*
  unemployment in, 38*f,* 40, 41*f,* 140, 140*f,* 151*t*
  welfare system model in, 157, 161–163
  well-established social partnerships in, 143, 148*t*

Bank bailouts, x
Belgium, 45*f,* 47*f,* 146
  employment in, 140, 141*f,* 142*t*
  EPL in, 48*f,* 162*t*
  LMPs of, 154*t,* 155, 156*t,* 157, 158*t*–159*t*
  STC in, 10, 52*f,* 120, 123–125, 124*t*
  STW in, 52*f,* 147, 148*t*
  UI in, 46*f,* 123
  unemployment in, 38*f,* 40, 41*f,* 140, 140*f,* 151*t*

welfare system model in, 157, 161–163
well-established social partnerships in, 143, 148*t*
Berkeley Planning Associates, STC study by, 127, 130*n*12
Born, Brooksley, envisioned film role for, xiii
Brazil, reversing income inequality in, xiv–xv
Brown, Sen. Sherrod, 128
Bulgaria
  employment in, 141*f,* 142*t,* 146
  LMPs of, 154*t,* 156*t,* 158*t*–159*t*
  unemployment in, 140*f,* 151*t*
Bush, Pres. George H.W., administration, xi

California
  STC requirements in, 131*t,* 133–134, 135*t*
  unemployment trend in, 117, 117*t,* 135*t*
Canada, 45*f,* 47*f*
  EPL in, 46, 48*f*
  STC in, 10, 52*f,* 120, 121, 124–125, 124*t,* 130*n*7
  UI in, 46*f,* 130*n*7
  unemployment in, 38*f,* 40, 41*f*
Cayman Islands, as tax haven, xiii
China, reversing income inequality in, xv
Clinton, Pres. William J., administration, xiii
Collective bargaining agreements, 53, 57, 143
  OECD countries with, 45, 47*f,* 120
Connecticut, STC requirements in, 116, 130*n*3, 131*t,* 133–134, 135*t*
Corporate policy
  flexible work-time arrangements as, 28, 29–30

Corporate policy, *cont.*
  government cooperation as, 95–96, 98
  recessions and, xiv, 7, 28, 29–30, 54
  *See also* Employers
Credit, layoff prevention and, 18
Cyprus
  employment in, 141*f,* 142*t*
  LMPs of, 154*t,* 156*t,* 158*t*–159*t*
  unemployment in, 140*f,* 151*t*
Czech Republic
  employment in, 141*f,* 142*t*
  EPL in, 146, 162*t*
  LMPs of, 154*t,* 156*t,* 158*t*–159*t*
  unemployment in, 140*f,* 147, 151*t*

Denmark
  ALMPs in, 44–45, 45*f,* 48, 54, 59*n*10
  employment in, 47–49, 50*f,* 52*f,* 141*f,*
    142*t*
  EPL in, 44, 45–46, 48*f,* 162*t*
  flexicurity in, 157, 160*t,* 161
  LMPs of, 8, 43–50, 56, 58, 154*t,* 156*t,*
    158*t*–159*t*
  UI in, 43, 44, 45, 46*f,* 59*n*9, 59*n*11,
    161
  unemployment in, 38*f,* 39, 40–41, 41*f,*
    43, 46–47, 49*f,* 51, 139, 140*f,* 151*t*
  workforce with collective bargaining
    agreements in, 45, 47*f*
Derivatives market, ix–x, xiii
Disability insurance, layoffs and, 20
Durbin, Sen. Richard, 128

Economic growth, xiv, 2, 6
  work-sharing policies and, xv, 9–10
Educational achievement, 3, 5–6, 19, 21
Employers
  policies to increase hiring by, 9,
    95–96
  recession responses by, 7, 18, 122
  STC by, 9–10, 53, 53*t,* 120, 148–149,
    164
  as UI claims agent, 115, 126, 130*n*11
Employment
  reemployment after nonemployment,
    21, 63, 146, 150

  reintegrating unemployed into, 10,
    20–21
  restoration of full, xiv–xv, xvi, 7–8
  stabilizing, with STC, 113–135
  *See also under names of countries,*
    *regions or states*
Employment protection legislation (EPL)
  flexicurity and, 157, 160*t,* 161
  as labor market rigidity, 42–43, 57
  in OECD 2008 countries, 45–46, 48*f,*
    56, 162*t*
Employment services
  public and private, 146, 152–153,
    153*t,* 160*t*
  social service agencies as, 9, 95–96
EPL. *See* Employment protection
    legislation
Estonia, 162*t*
  employment in, 139, 141*f,* 142*t,* 153*t*
  LMPs of, 154*t,* 156*t,* 158*t*–159*t*
  unemployment in, 139, 140*f,* 151*t*
EU member states. *See* European Union
European Central Bank, interest rates
    and, 39
European Union (EU), 10, 162*t*
  employment in, 138, 139, 141*f,* 142*t*
  GDP in, 138, 142*t*
  LMPs of, 137, 154*t,* 155–157, 156*t,*
    158*t*–159*t,* 160*t,* 163–165, 165*n*1
  unemployment in, 138–139, 140*f,*
    154*t,* 156t
  *See also names of individual member*
    *states, e.g.,* Belgium

Family income of job losers
  children and, 3–4, 17, 20, 27–28
Federal Reserve Board, interest rates
    and, 38–39
Financial health, 21
  post–job loss, of workers, 3, 5, 17, 18
  recessionary earnings losses and,
    19–20, 30
Financial sector
  expected *vs.* unexpected behaviors of,
    xi–xii
  Glass-Steagall repeal and, ix–x

Financial sector, *cont.*
  trust in, and well-functioning
    economy, xiii–xiv
  *See also* Wall Street
Finland, 45*f,* 47*f*
  employment in, 52*f,* 141*f,* 142*t*
  EPL in, 48*f,* 162*t*
  flexicurity in, 157, 160*t,* 161
  LMPs of, 154*t,* 156*t,* 158*t*–159*t*
  unemployed income support in, 46*f,*
    147, 151*t*
  unemployment in, 38*f,* 40, 41*f,* 140*f*
Flexicurity, 43–44, 54, 120, 157, 160*t,*
    161, 163–165
Florida
  STC requirements in, 131*t,* 133–134,
    135*t*
  unemployment trend in, 117, 117*t,*
    135*t*
France, 45*f,* 47*f,* 146
  employment in, 52*f,* 141*f,* 142*t,* 153*t*
  EPL in, 46, 48*f,* 162*t*
  LMPs of, 154*t,* 156*t,* 158*t*–159*t*
  STW in, 52*f,* 147, 148*t*
  unemployed income support in, 46*f,*
    147, 151*t*
  unemployment in, 38*f,* 40, 41*f,* 140*f*

GDP. *See* Gross Domestic Product
Geisel, Theodor Seuss (pseud. Dr.
  Seuss),
    economic perspectives in
    children's books of, viii–ix, xi–
    xvi, 8
Gekko, Gordon (film character), xii,
  xviin5
*General theory of employment, interest
  and money, The* (Keynes), 41
Germany, 21, 45*f,* 58*n*2
  employment in, 51–52, 51*f,* 53*t,* 55,
    140, 141*f,* 142*t*
  EPL in, 46, 48*f,* 53, 162*t*
  LMPs of, 8–9, 50–54, 57, 58, 59*n*12,
    154*t,* 155, 156*t,* 157, 158*t*–159*t*
  public employment services offered
    in, 146, 153*t*

STC in, 10, 28–29, 31*n*12, 113, 120,
    121–122, 124–125, 124*t*
STW as STC in, 51–53, 52*f,* 53*t,* 54,
    59*n*13, 147, 148*t*
UI in, 45, 46*f,* 126–127, 130*n*12
unemployment in, 37–39, 38*f,* 40–41,
    41*f,* 46–47, 49*f,* 50–51, 58, 122,
    140, 140*f,* 151*t*
welfare system model in, 157, 161–
    163
well-established social partnerships
    in, 143, 148*t*
work-time accounts in, 29, 31*n*13, 53,
    53*t,* 59*nn*14–15, 120, 122
workforce with collective bargaining
    agreements in, 45, 47*f*
Glass-Steagall Act, repeal of, ix–x
Global Jobs Pact, 137, 165*n*1
Greece, 45*f,* 46*f,* 47*f*
  employment in, 141*f,* 142*t,* 153*t*
  EPL in, 48*f,* 162*t*
  LMPs of, 154*t,* 156*t,* 158*t*–159*t*
  unemployment in, 38*f,* 40, 41*f,* 140*f,*
    151*t*
Greed, job losses and, xii
Greenspan, Alan, xiii
Grinch, The (Seuss character), viii–ix,
  xi–xiii
Gross domestic product (GDP)
  2008–10, change in EU, 138, 139*f,*
    142*t*
  decline in, and unemployment, 7,
    8–9, 38–39, 57–58, 113
  economic growth and, 2, 10
Gross national product, decline in, 63

Horton (Seuss character), xiii–xvi
Hortonomics, as investment, xiii–xv
Housing market, recession vulnerability
    and, 42, 58*n*2
Hungary, 162*t*
  employment in, 141*f,* 142*t*
  LMPs of, 154*t,* 156*t,* 158*t*–159*t*
  STW in, 52*f,* 147, 148*t*
  unemployment in, 140*f,* 151*t*

Income inequality
  financial sector and, ix–xi
  global, compared to U.S., vii, xvin1
  Occupy Wall Street protesters and,
    xv–xvi
  reversing trend in, xiv–xv
  Seuss insight to, viii–ix, xi–xvi, xvin2
Institute for Research on Labor and
    Employment, UCLA, 6–7
  conference presentations at, 7–11
Interest rates, macroeconomic policy
    and, 38–39, 58n4
International Labour Conference, Global
    Jobs Pact adopted by, 137, 165n1
Investment, xiii–xv, 57–58
Iowa, STC requirements in, 116, 130n3,
    131t, 133–134, 135t
Ireland, 45f, 46f
  employment in, 52f, 139, 141f, 142t
  EPL in, 46, 48f, 162t
  LMPs of, 154t, 156t, 158t–159t
  unemployment in, 37, 38f, 40, 41f,
    138, 140f, 151t
Italy, 45f, 47f, 146
  employment in, 52f, 140, 141f, 142t
  EPL in, 48f, 162t
  LMPs of, 154t, 155, 156t, 157,
    158t–159t
  STW in, 52f, 147, 148t
  unemployed income support in, 46f,
    147, 151t
  unemployment in, 38f, 40, 41f, 140,
    140f
  welfare system model in, 157, 161–
    163
  well-established social partnerships
    in, 143, 148t

Japan, 45f, 47f
  employment in, 48f, 52f
  unemployment in, 38f, 40, 41f, 46f
Job creation, xiii
  policies to increase, 7, 9, 144t–145t,
    146, 150
  tax incentives for, 25, 128–129
Job losses, xii

bank bailouts vs., x–xi
  crisis in, across all groups, viii, 1,
    10–11
  effects of, 3–6, 17–21, 30, 30n1, 63
    (see also under Unemployment,
    health effects of)
  mortality and, xvin4, 20
  Occupy Wall Street protesters and,
    xv–xvi
  reversing trend in, xiv–xv, 1–2, 6, 8
  See also Corporate policy; Public
    policy
Job preservation
  productivity trade-off for, xiv–xv
  STC for, 9–10, 144t–145t, 147–149,
    148t
  training and, 8, 10, 22, 26
  work sharing for, 125–126, 130n1
  worker mobility for, 26–27, 146
Just-world hypothesis, 100, 102, 104,
    108–109

Kansas
  STC requirements in, 131t, 133–134,
    135t
  unemployment trend in, 117, 117t,
    135t
Keynes, John Maynard, 41
Kurzarbeit. See under Germany, STC in

Labor force, 2–3, 6, 11n1, 27
  See also Workforce
Labor market measures in crisis, 137–165
  effectiveness of, 149–153, 153t
  effectiveness of social models as,
    157, 161–163, 162t
  EU policies adapted or adopted, 137,
    155–157, 158t–159t, 160t, 165n1
  European anticrisis measures, 142–
    149, 144t–145t, 148t
  figures of crisis, 138–142, 139f, 140f,
    141f, 142t
  framing the issue, 137–138
  lesson from the crisis, 163–165
  public spending on policies for, 153–
    155, 154f, 156f, 165n2

Labor market policy (LMP)
    Denmark, in the Great Recession,
        43–50
    EU countries and variations of (*see*
        *under* Labor market measures in
        crisis, European anticrisis
        measures)
    GDP decline and, effect on jobs, 8–9,
        38–39
    Germany, in the Great Recession,
        50–54
    lessons for the U.S. from OECD
        member states in, 54–58
    OECD member states, in the Great
        Recession, 37–54
    *See also* Active labor market policies
        (ALMPs)
Labor markets
    macroeconomic shocks and, 40–42,
        41*f*, 48, 57, 113
    rigidities in, 42–43
Latin America, reversing income
        inequality in, xiv–xv
Latvia
    employment in, 139, 141*f*, 142*t*
    LMPs of, 154*t*, 156*t*, 158*t*–159*t*
    unemployed income support in, 147,
        151*t*
    unemployment in, 139, 140*f*
Layoffs, 43, 126
    consequences of, 19–20, 160*t*
    options to prevent, in recessions, 18,
        28–30, 31*n*12, 125, 130*n*5
    reasons for earnings losses after,
        21–23, 30–31*n*2
    reduced hours *vs.*, 7, 8, 9–10, 18, 52,
        53, 56, 114
Levitt, Arthur, xiii
Lithuania
    employment in, 139, 141*f*, 142*t*
    LMPs of, 146, 154*t*, 156*t*, 158*t*–159*t*
    unemployment in, 139, 140*f*, 151*t*
LMP. *See* Labor market policy
Luxembourg
    employment in, 141*f*, 142*t*, 153*t*, 162*t*

    LMPs of, 154*t*, 155, 156*t*, 158*t*–159*t*
    unemployment in, 140*f*, 151*t*

Madoff, Bernard, resemblance of, ix, xii
Malta
    employment in, 141*f*, 142*t*
    LMPs of, 154*t*, 156*t*, 158*t*–159*t*
    unemployment in, 140*f*, 151*t*
Marital health, worker post–job loss and,
        5, 20
Maryland
    STC requirements in, 131*t*, 133–134,
        135*t*
    unemployment trend in, 117, 117*t*,
        135*t*
Massachusetts, STC requirements in,
        131*t*, 133–134, 135*t*
Mental health
    causality data and methodology, 64,
        66–68, 80*nn*6–7
    conclusion, 78–80
    descriptive statistics, 68–71, 80*n*8,
        82*t*–83*t*, 84*t*–85*t*
    empirical procedures, 71–73
    mediative-buffer link question, 75–
        78, 82*t*–83*t*, 90*t*
    unemployment and psychological
        distress, 73–75, 86*t*–87*t*, 88*t*–89*t*
    unemployment as causality of, xi,
        xvi*n*4, 4–5, 9, 63–66, 80*nn*1–5
Middle Class Tax Relief and Job
        Creation Act, U.S., 114, 128–129
Minnesota, STC requirements in, 116,
        130*n*3, 131*t*, 133–134, 135*t*
Missouri
    STC requirements in, 131*t*, 133–134,
        135*t*
    unemployment trend in, 117, 117*t*,
        135*t*

National Comorbidity Survey
        Replication (NCS-R), causality
        data from, 64, 66, 69*t*, 70, 74*t*,
        76*t*–77*t*, 79*t*, 84*t*–85*t*, 86*t*–87*t*,
        88*t*–89*t*

National Latino and Asian American
    Study (NLAAS), causality data
    from, 64, 66, 69*t*, 70, 74*t*, 76*t*–77*t*,
    79*t*, 84*t*–85*t*, 86*t*–87*t*, 88*t*–89*t*
NCS-R. *See* National Comorbidity
    Survey Replication
Netherlands, The, 45*f*, 46*f*, 47*f*
    employment in, 52*f*, 140, 141*f*, 142*t*
    EPL in, 48*f*, 162*t*
    flexicurity in, 157, 160*t*, 161
    LMPs of, 154*t*, 155, 156*t*, 158*t*–159*t*
    private employment services offered
        in, 146, 153*t*
    STW in, 52*f*, 147, 148*t*, 157
    unemployment in, 38*f*, 40, 41*f*, 95,
        140, 140*f*, 151*t*
    well-established social partnerships
        in, 143, 148*t*
    work sharing in, 95–110
New York (State), STC requirements in,
    131*t*, 133–134, 135*t*
New Zealand, 45*f*, 46*f*, 47*f*, 52*f*
    EPL in, 46, 48*f*
    unemployment in, 38*f*, 40, 41*f*
NLAAS. *See* National Latino and Asian
    American Study
Norway, 45*f*, 46*f*, 47*f*
    employment in, 48*f*, 52*f*, 146
    flexicurity in, 157, 160*t*, 161
    unemployment in, 38*f*, 40, 41*f*

Obama, Pres. Barack, administration, xi,
    57–58
    stimulus package of, x–xi, xvi*n*3
Occupy Wall Street protesters, national
    issues discourse and, xv–xvi
OECD member states. *See* Organisation
    for Economic Co-operation and
    Development
Okun's Law, 63
Once-ler, The (Seuss character), xii, xiii
Oregon, STC requirements in, 131*t*,
    133–134, 135*t*
Organisation for Economic Co-operation
    and Development (OECD)

collective bargaining agreements in,
    47*f*, 120
EPL 2008 in, 45–46, 48*f*
job preservation policies in, xiv–xv
labor markets and macroeconomic
    shocks in, 40–42, 41*f*
LMPs of, in the Great Recession,
    37–39, 42–54, 113, 120, 163
STW in, 52*f*, 149
unemployment rates in, 37–39, 38*f*
*See also names of individual member
    states, e.g.,* Denmark

Pay for performance, tax code incentive
    and, xiii, xvii*n*6
Physical health, stress-related, xi, xvi*n*4,
    4, 20
Poland
    employment in, 141*f*, 142*t*, 162*t*
    LMPs of, 154*t*, 156*t*, 158*t*–159*t*
    STW in, 52*f*, 147, 148*t*
    unemployment in, 140*f*, 147, 151*t*
Political environment, policy approaches
    amid fraught, 10–11
Portugal, 45*f*
    employment in, 47*f*, 141*f*, 142*t*
    EPL in, 48*f*, 162*t*
    LMPs of, 146, 154*t*, 156*t*, 158*t*–159*t*
    unemployment in, 38*f*, 40, 41*f*, 140*f*,
        151*t*
Poverty, U.S. rates of, 4, 21
Productivity, xiv–xv, 58*n*5
Public assistance, 18
    job search counseling as, 26, 31*n*9,
        151*t*
    in job training and employment, 25,
        31*nn*7–8, 43, 146
Public policy
    adapted or adopted by EU, 137, 155–
        157, 158*t*–159*t*, 160*t*, 165*n*1
    fiscal stimuli, 27, 39, 58*n*3
    long-term unemployment reduction
        in, 25–28
    recessions and, xiv–xv, 7, 18, 23–29,
        38–39
    subsidies in, 25, 27, 31*n*7, 31*n*10, 146

Public policy, *cont.*
  tax incentives in, xiii, xvii*n*6, 25
  UI in, 23–26, 31*nn*3–6, 57, 59*n*19,
    114, 126–127, 128

Reagan, Pres. Ronald, administration, xi
Recessions, 42, 58*nn*1–2
  policy options and, xiv–xv, 7, 10,
    23–30
  socioeconomic scarring and, 3–6
  U.S., and job losses, 1–3
Reed, Sen. Jack, 128
Retirement plans, xiii, xvii*n*6, 6
Rhode Island, 126
  duration of STC and regular UI in,
    119, 133
  STC requirements in, 116, 130*n*3,
    131*t*, 133–134, 135*t*
  unemployment trend in, 117, 117*t*,
    135*t*
Romania
  employment in, 141*f*, 142*t*
  LMPs of, 154*t*, 156*t*, 158*t*–159*t*
  unemployment in, 140*f*, 147, 151*t*
Roosevelt, Pres. Franklin D.,
    administration, xi
Rubin, Robert, xiii

Seuss, Dr. *See* Geisel, Theodor Seuss
Short-time compensation (STC)
    programs, xiv, 9–10, 113–135
  analysis of, in U.S., 52*f*, 56, 116–119,
    130*n*3, 130*n*6, 131*t*, 133–134, 135*t*
  international comparison of, 120–125,
    124*t*, 149–150
  layoff prevention through, 18, 28–29,
    31*nn*11–12, 114, 130*n*1
  options for, increase in U.S., 125–
    129, 130*nn*10–12
  STW as, in Germany, 51–53, 52*f*, 53*t*,
    54, 59*n*13, 160*t*, 164
  work-sharing as, 95–110, 113, 114,
    130*n*1
Short-time work programs. *See under*
    Short-time compensation (STC)
    programs, STW as

Slovakia, 140*f*, 146
  employment in, 141*f*, 142*t*, 162*t*
  LMPs of, 154*t*, 156*t*, 158*t*–159*t*
  STW in, 52*f*, 147, 148*t*
Slovenia
  employment in, 141*f*, 142*t*, 153*t*, 162*t*
  LMPs of, 146, 154*t*, 156*t*, 158*t*–159*t*
  unemployment in, 140*f*, 151*t*
Social mobility, vii, viii, xvi*n*1
Social models. *See* Flexicurity; Welfare
    system
Social responsibility, companies and, 98,
    100, 103, 107, 109
Social service agencies, 109
  cooperation of employers with, 9,
    95–96
  predicting cooperation of employers
    with (*see* Theory of planned
    behavior)
Socioeconomic factors, 6
  global *vs.* U.S. conditions and, vii,
    xvi*n*1
  scarring by, during recessions, 3–6, 9
Spain, 45*f*, 46*f*
  employment in, 47*f*, 52*f*, 139, 141*f*,
    142*t*, 146
  EPL in, 48*f*, 162*t*
  GDP in, 40, 41*f*, 142*t*
  LMPs of, 154*t*, 156*t*, 158*t*–159*t*
  unemployment in, 37, 38*f*, 40, 41*f*,
    46–47, 49*f*, 138, 140*f*, 151*t*
STC programs. *See* Short-time
    compensation programs
STW (Short-time work) programs. *See*
    *under* Short-time compensation
    programs, STW as
Subsidies, 146, 150
  wages supported by, 25, 27, 31*n*7,
    31*n*10
Summers, Larry, xiii
Sweden, 45*f*, 46*f*, 47*f*
  employment in, 141*f*, 142*t*
  EPL in, 46, 48*f*, 162*t*
  flexicurity in, 157, 160*t*, 161
  LMPs of, 146, 154*t*, 156*t*, 158*t*–159*t*

Sweden, *cont.*
 unemployment in, 38*f,* 40, 41*f,* 140*f,*
  147, 151*t*
Switzerland, 45*f,* 46*f*
 employment in, 47*f,* 48*f,* 52*f*
 unemployment in, 38*f,* 40, 41*f*

TARP. *See* Troubled Asset Relief
 Program
Tax havens, profit in, xiii
Tax incentives, 127, 146
 for job creation, 25, 128–129
 modification of corporate, xiii,
  xviin6
 temporary work hour reductions, 57,
  113–114
Taxes, personal, 115, 130*n*2
Texas, STC requirements in, 131*t,* 133–
 134, 135*t*
Theory of planned behavior, 96–101
 behavioral beliefs in, 97–98, 102,
  103*t*
 company size and, 96, 100–101,
  103–106, 105*t,* 109–110
 just-world hypothesis, 100, 102, 104,
  108–109
 predictive power and implications of,
  107–109
 subjective norms in, 97, 98, 102,
  107–108
Trade-offs, xiv–xv, 39
Trade unions
 collective bargaining of, in OECD
  countries, 47*f,* 53, 56, 120
 in Denmark, 43–44, 45, 59*n*9
 labor market rigidities and, 42–43
 STC plans for U.S. and, 126, 130*n*10
Troubled Asset Relief Program (TARP),
 x–xi

UI. *See* Unemployment insurance
Underemployment, socioeconomic
 scarring and, 3
Unemployment
 consequences of, in recessions, 17–23
 GDP 2007–09 and, 39, 40, 41*f*

health effects of, xi, xvi*n*4, 4–5, 7, 8,
 9, 17, 20
 (*see also under* Mental health)
 impacts on workers of, 3–5
 income support measures for, 144*t,*
  146–147, 150–151
 long-term, and policies to address it,
  7–11, 56–57, 59*n*18, 80, 82
 seasonal adjustments and, 2, 11*n*2
 U.S. rates of, 2–3, 9, 10, 38*f,* 116–
  118, 117*t*
 *See also under names of countries,*
  *regions or states*
Unemployment insurance (UI), 18, 46*f,*
 52
 cost of benefits for, 10, 18–19, 30,
  119, 128–129
 employer-filed claims for, 115, 126,
  130*n*11
 exhaustion of, benefits, 21, 127–128
 labor market rigidities and, 42–43
 partial, and state agency requirements
  for STC, 115–116, 131*t,* 133–134,
  135*t*
 as public policy, 23–26, 31*nn*3–6, 57,
  59*n*19, 114, 127, 128, 160*t*
 recipient obligations for, 150–151,
  151*t*
United Kingdom (U.K.), 45*f,* 46*f*
 employment in, 47*f,* 141*f,* 142*t,* 146,
  153*t*
 EPL in, 46, 48*f,* 162*t*
 LMPs of, 146, 154*t,* 156*t,* 158*t*–159*t*
 unemployment in, 38*f,* 40, 41*f,* 140*f,*
  151*t*
United States (U.S.), x, 45*f,* 58*n*2
 employment and hours 2007–09 in,
  55–56, 55*f,* 59*n*16
 poverty rates in, 4, 21
 presidential administrations of, x–xi,
  xi, xvi*n*3, 57–58
 socioeconomic conditions in, *vs.*
  global, vii, xvi*n*1, 29
 STC analysis in, 52*f,* 56, 116–119,
  123–125, 124*t,* 130*n*3, 130*n*6,
  130*nn*8–9, 131*t,* 133–134, 135*t*

United States (U.S.), *cont.*
    STC in, *vs.* global, xiv, 10, 28, 57,
        59*n*17
    STC options for increase in, 125–129,
        130*nn*10–12
    UI in, 45, 46*f,* 115–116
    unemployment in, 37–39, 38*f,* 39,
        40–41, 41*f,* 46–47, 49*f,* 57–58,
        125
    workforce percentage with collective
        bargaining agreements in, 45, 47*f,*
        56
    *See also names of individual member*
        *states, e.g.,* Rhode Island
U.S. Congress, testimony
    House Committee on Financial
        Services, 28, 31*n*11
    Joint Economic Committee, 30
U.S. Department of Labor, proposed STC
    responsibilities of, 129
U.S. law and legislation, 126
    employment protection in, 46, 48*f*
    increasing STC programs, 114, 128–
        129
    repeals of, ix–x
University of California, Los Angeles,
    Institute for Research on Labor
    and Employment at, 6–7

Vermont
    duration of STC and regular UI in,
        119, 133
    STC requirements in, 131*t,* 133–134,
        135*t*
    unemployment trend in, 117, 117*t,*
        135*t*

Wages
    cuts in, and demand, 40–42, 58*n*5
    effect of unemployment on, 3–4
    reemployment, after nonemployment,
        21, 63
Wall Street
    Grinches of, ix–xiii
    implosion of, x–xi, xvi
    occupation protesters and, xv

WARN legislation, 126
Washington (State)
    STC requirements in, 131*t,* 133–134,
        135*t*
    unemployment trend in, 117*t,* 118,
        135*t*
Welfare system, 157, 160*t,* 161–163,
    164–165
Who, A (Seuss character), in Who-ville,
    xi, xiii, xv–xvi
Work-sharing approaches. *See* Short-time
    compensation programs
Work-time arrangements, layoff
    prevention and, 18, 29, 31*n*12
Workforce, 5, 47*f*
    age of, 6, 21, 22
    effects of economy on, 3–4, 8, 18
    mobility of, 19–20, 22, 26–27, 146
    options for, upon declines in demand,
        xiv–xv, 7
    psychological resilience *vs.*
        vulnerability of, 66–67, 68–71,
        69*t,* 79–80, 82*t,* 84*t*–85*t,* 90*t*
    (*see also* Mental health)
World trade, recession vulnerability and,
    58*n*2

# About the Institute

The W.E. Upjohn Institute for Employment Research is a nonprofit research organization devoted to finding and promoting solutions to employment-related problems at the national, state, and local levels. It is an activity of the W.E. Upjohn Unemployment Trustee Corporation, which was established in 1932 to administer a fund set aside by Dr. W.E. Upjohn, founder of The Upjohn Company, to seek ways to counteract the loss of employment income during economic downturns.

The Institute is funded largely by income from the W.E. Upjohn Unemployment Trust, supplemented by outside grants, contracts, and sales of publications. Activities of the Institute comprise the following elements: 1) a research program conducted by a resident staff of professional social scientists; 2) a competitive grant program, which expands and complements the internal research program by providing financial support to researchers outside the Institute; 3) a publications program, which provides the major vehicle for disseminating the research of staff and grantees, as well as other selected works in the field; and 4) an Employment Management Services division, which manages most of the publicly funded employment and training programs in the local area.

The broad objectives of the Institute's research, grant, and publication programs are to 1) promote scholarship and experimentation on issues of public and private employment and unemployment policy, and 2) make knowledge and scholarship relevant and useful to policymakers in their pursuit of solutions to employment and unemployment problems.

Current areas of concentration for these programs include causes, consequences, and measures to alleviate unemployment; social insurance and income maintenance programs; compensation; workforce quality; work arrangements; family labor issues; labor-management relations; and regional economic development and local labor markets.